The Economics of Technical Information Systems

J. N. Wolfe
with the assistance of
**Thomas M. Aitchison
Donald H. Brydon
Alexander Scott
Ralph Young**

The Praeger Special Studies program—utilizing the most modern and efficient book production techniques and a selective worldwide distribution network—makes available to the academic, government, and business communities significant, timely research in U.S. and international economic, social, and political development.

The Economics of Technical Information Systems

PRAEGER SPECIAL STUDIES IN INTERNATIONAL ECONOMICS AND DEVELOPMENT

Praeger Publishers New York Washington London

Library of Congress Cataloging in Publication Data

Wolfe, James N
  The economics of technical information systems.

  (Praeger special studies in international economics and development)
    1. Technology—Information services—Great Britain.
  2. Communication of technical information. 3. Cost effectiveness. I. Aitchison, Thomas Morton. II. Title.
  T10.65.G7W64   607   72-170278

PRAEGER PUBLISHERS
111 Fourth Avenue, New York, N.Y. 10003, U.S.A.
5, Cromwell Place, London SW7 2JL, England

Published in the United States of America in 1974
by Praeger Publishers, Inc.

All rights reserved

© 1974 by Praeger Publishers, Inc.

Printed in the United States of America

PREFACE

The present study was begun in October 1967 at the request of the Office for Scientific and Technical Information (OSTI), a branch of the Department of Education and Science of the United Kingdom. It has had the support of the Organization for Economic Cooperation and Development (OECD), which is actively pursuing studies into the possibilities of international cooperation in the field of information.

The study was conducted by a team recruited by the Department of Economics of the University of Edinburgh, but it has been throughout an interdisciplinary team composed of statisticians, mathematicians, accountants, and information specialists, as well as economists.

The study combined the work of a number of part-time staff, mainly engaged in academic teaching responsibilities, with the work of a group of full-time staff, employed as research associates within the Department of Economics. The length of the project (three years) and the fluidity of the academic market have meant that the team has had a different composition at different times and that only a part of the team was employed on the project for the full three-year period. These permutations of full- and part-time employment, and of comings and goings, make it rather difficult to assign credits in an altogether satisfactory way. It may be helpful to mention that D. H. Brydon, A. Scott and R. Young were engaged on the project full time throughout. Others engaged full time on the project for varying periods included Dr. J. Moreh (now of Queen's University, Belfast) and Miss A. Mackney. Among those engaged on a part-time basis were T. M. Aitchison of the Institute of Electrical Engineers, who acted as information consultant; P. R. Fisk of the Department of Statistics of the University of Edinburgh, who acted as statistical consultant; W. D. C. Wright of the Department of Economics; and the director, Professor J. N. Wolfe. Those contributing included M. Allingham and I. Smith, Professor J. T. Romans and Dr. L. C. Wright of the Department of Economics, and Mr. W. Bishop, a partner in Wallace and Somerville, Accountants.

The study has benefited from advice and consultation from a number of eminent economists specializing in particular theoretical points touched on in the study. Among these must be mentioned Professor C. Blake of Dundee University, Professor W. M. Gorman of the London School of Economics, Monsieur Edmond Malinvaud of Institut Nationale de la Statistique et des Edudes Economiques in Paris, and Professor Alan Walters of the London School of Economics.

CONTENTS

	Page
PREFACE	v
LIST OF TABLES	ix
LIST OF FIGURES	xii

Chapter

1	BACKGROUND	1
2	THEORY	11

    The Nature of Cost-Benefit Analysis   15
    Internal Versus External Costs and
        Benefits   18
    Estimating Benefits   18
    External Benefits   21
    The Wessel and Moore Report   21
        Score Analysis   22
        Scout Analysis   23
        Core Analysis   24
        Game Analysis   25
    Notes   25

3	THE STUDY	27

    Grading   27
    Characteristics   30
    Effectiveness Questionnaire   33
    Possible Amendments   37
    Weighting   38
    Aggregation and Classification of Second-
        ary Information Services   39
    Stratification   40
    Costing Measurements   41
        Costs   41

Chapter		Page
	Notes	43
	Appendix to Chapter 3: The Sample	43
4	RESULTS	61
	Effectiveness Results	61
	Measures of Effectiveness and Dependence	63
	Average Individual Values	63
	Effectiveness Measures and Information Need	66
	Effectiveness Measures and Type of Work	66
	Effectiveness Measures and Age of Respondents	66
	Effectiveness Measures and Salary	70
	Effectiveness Measures and Years Spent in Research and Development	70
	Effectiveness Measures and Respondent's Discipline	70
	Breakdown by Industry and Type of Service	72
	Analysis of Cost Results	84
	United Kingdom Expenditure on Secondary Information Systems	85
	Costs in Detail	86
	The Cost of an Abstract	88
	Amalgamation of Secondary Information Systems	90
	Overhead Costs	91
	Cost-Effectiveness Measures	91
	Other Results	95
	Method 1. Average System	97
	Method 2. Information-Conscious System	97
	Method 3. Reasonable Budget System	98
	Method 4. Constant Rate of Surplus System	98
	Summary and Conclusions	101
	Notes	102
5	CONCLUSIONS	103
APPENDIX		
A	THE QUESTIONNAIRE	110

Appendix	Page
B SAMPLE FRAME	129
C COST MANUAL	130
D INFORMATION EFFECTIVENESS STUDY MANUAL	147
ABOUT THE CONTRIBUTORS	168

LIST OF TABLES

Table		Page
3.1	The Distribution of the Sample by Industry	44
3.2	Total Individual Respondents by Industry	44
3.3	Individual Respondents by Method of Selection	45
3.4	Value of A, B, and D Values and X-Factor Secondary Information, by Method of Selection	45
3.5	Sample of Individual Respondents by Field of Interest	46
3.6	Average Salaries of R & D Workers by Industry	50
3.7	Average Salary per Discipline Group	51
3.8	Average Number of Years in Research and Development and Mean Age of Each Respondent, by Industry and Large/Small Firm	54
3.9	Number of Years in Research and Development, by Discipline	55
3.10	Average Percentage of Total Time Spent on Research and Development, by Industry	57
3.11	Percentage Time Spent on Research and Development, by Dicipline	57
3.12	Information Expenditure and R & D Effort	59
4.1	The Relationship between the Value of Published Secondary Information and Other Sources of Secondary Information Displayed with Respect to the Type of Information Need	63
4.2	The Relationship between the Value of Published Secondary Information and Other Sources of Secondary Information Displayed with Respect to the Discipline of the Respondents	64

Table		Page
4.3	The Relationship between the Value of Published Secondary Information and Other Sources of Secondary Information Displayed with Respect to the Industry Classifications	65
4.4	Different Measures Displayed with Respect to Information Need	67
4.5	Different Measures Displayed with Respect to Type of Work	67
4.6	Different Measures Displayed with Respect to Age of Respondents	68
4.7	Different Measures Displayed with Respect to Salary	68
4.8	Different Measures Displayed with Respect to Years Spent in Research and Development	69
4.9	Different Measures Displayed with Respect to Discipline	69
4.10	Aggregate Effectiveness Values per Industry	71
4.11	Average Effectiveness Values per Firm in Each Industry	71
4.12	Average Effectiveness Values per Individual in Each Industry	74
4.13	Average Effectiveness Values per Firm Classified by Information-Conscious and Other Firms, between Industries	76
4.14	Average Effectiveness Values per Individual in Information-Conscious and Other Firms, by Industry	78
4.15	Average Effectiveness Values per Individual by Type of Service and Ranking of Selected Measures	79

Table		Page
4.16	Average Effectiveness Values per Individual by Type of Service in Information-Conscious and Other Firms, by Industry	80
4.17	Average Characteristic Effectiveness Values per Individual by Type of Service	83
4.18	Information Systems: Size Distribution	86
4.19	Production of Abstracts—Costs in Index Form	87
4.20	The Relationship Between Cost per Abstract and Index of Length and Number Produced	90
4.21	Aggregate Effectiveness Values	93
4.22	Aggregated C_1, E_1, and Dependence Index Weighted by Cost of Service and Ranked	94
4.23	All Firms: Information Expenditure per R & D Worker	97
4.24	Information-Conscious Firms: Information Expenditure per R & D Worker	98
4.25	Reasonable Information Expenditure per R & D Worker	99
4.26	Estimates of Suitable Expenditure per R & D Worker	101

LIST OF FIGURES

Figure		
2.1	Hypothetical Evaluation of an Information Service	17
3.1	Distribution of Salary	49
3.2	Distribution among Respondents of Age	52

Figure		Page
3.3	Salary and Age of Respondents	53
3.4	Distribution among Respondents of Time Spent on Research and Development	56
3.5	Time Spent on Information Work Related to Time Spent on Research and Development	58
3.6	Relationship between R & D Time Spent on Information and Information Time Spent on Secondary Information	58

APPENDIX FIGURE

C.1	Flow Chart: Abstracts Services, Production of Monthly Abstract Journal	143

The Economics of Technical Information Systems

CHAPTER

1

BACKGROUND

    It is one of the central features of the development of the modern industrial state that an increasing proportion of its activities is coming within the scope of what has been called the "grant economy." An increasing range of goods and services is provided to the public by the state or by grant-financed institutions either free or on the basis of nominal payment. The demand for the output from this grant sector of the economy is naturally high and tends to be rapidly increasing. As the grant sector of the economy grows, its various components compete for funds ever more fiercely among themselves, as well as against the private sector. At an early stage this competition takes the form of hortatory injunctions and appeals to higher feelings. But the performance of the grant economy has become so important to the level and growth of productivity in other sectors that it has become impossible to leave the outcome to such instruments. A recognition has emerged of the need for a rational distribution of resources to, and within, the grant sector on the basis of the quantitative analysis of the benefits accruing from expenditure in each of its parts. There is some danger in this development since certain benefits are more easily and quickly quantifiable than others. But many characteristics at first thought unquantifiable are seen on careful and thorough investigation to be subject to quantification. And the progress of research in this branch of economics has been so rapid that the errors made by ignoring the unquantifiable are probably now less than those made by attaching too much weight to it.
    In any event, the question of whether quantification should or should not be the basis for selection among areas in the grant economy is by now largely academic. Government and public alike increasingly demand such a justification, and the main way of defending the access to funds of any particular project is to provide quantified argumentation.

The use of such quantitative analysis need not be confined to governmental or foundation-supported projects. It is not sufficiently appreciated that many of the activities within the private firm are only indirectly subject to the discipline of prices or markets. A great deal of the staff and support work of the modern corporation has this character. Moreover, a service unit within the firm may be profitable when considered as a whole, but many of its detailed activities may be of little use. For example, the detailed conduct of information work within the firm is usually left to the discretion of information experts, and little effort seems to be made to ensure that the material provided by the information service renders value for money in every instance. Some informal techniques may be utilized to ensure that the information system is not grossly wasteful, but a full analysis of the system would in fact require something very much like a cost-benefit study. The practice in some companies of making the information agency dependent for funds upon allocations from operating departments does not in itself ensure the most efficient detailed operation of the information agency, unless each item of information service is priced separately.

The objective of the present volume is to develop a general methodology for the evaluation of services provided within a government department or business enterprise when the service is not sold at a price that covers its actual cost. The particular service we will be considering is that of the provision of nonprimary information. A detailed definition of this service will be provided later in this chapter. The service analyzed is a highly particular one, but a good deal of the methodology arising in this study has a wider application. Institutional details will of course differ in any extension, but it is felt that the principles at least may be revealing.

The development of nonprimary information services must be seen in the context of the expansion of R & D (research and development) activity over the past three or four decades. A great boost to this activity has been given by the wartime expansion and continued postwar plateau of defense expenditure and especially the great bursts of effort involved in nuclear and aerospace development. This R & D activity has indeed found an echo in purely commercial sectors, but it is clear that it is still highly sensitive to fluctuations in defense procurement activity. The development of nonprimary information services is to a considerable degree an adjunct of this R & D activity, although it would be wrong not to see this development as a potentially self-sustaining one whose value renders a regression to older information forms highly unlikely.

We intend to study how efficiently nonprimary information services are produced, and to what degree consumers' wants are satisfied. In this study we shall distinguish between several types and elements of information service in the following way. Those nonprimary information services provided within the firm or establishment (e.g., information offices or special libraries) will be called technical information services. Those nonprimary services provided by specialist information agencies outside the firm or establishment will be called secondary information services. The total nonprimary information activity encompassed in these two ways will be spoken of as the total secondary information service. It will be observed that a technical information service may make use of the activity of a secondary information service, but not normally the reverse.

There is, unfortunately, little readily available data covering the field in which we are interested. One of the objectives of the study, therefore, is the generation of relevant data. The scope of this study was necessarily confined to certain areas of activity. A number of British industries were selected for special study: chemicals, aircraft, and electrical engineering were selected for their high R & D content, textiles because of its traditionally low R & D effort, and agriculture because it is not a manufacturing industry in the same sense as the others but does have a certain amount of research and development. The basic population of users from which we estimate the effectiveness of secondary information is the total R & D personnel in each of these industries. This entailed the random selection of a number of firms in each industry up to a prescribed maximum and the random selection of a set number of R & D personnel within each firm that carried out research and development. The application of statistical techniques in this rather complex sampling and estimation situation constitutes one of the important aspects of the study.

It is a commonplace of information work to start with a general account of the so-called information explosion and to describe the massive increase in the publication of scientific and technical papers and reports that took place during and immediately following World War II and that has continued at an increasing pace ever since.

For present purposes it is sufficient to note that the sheer volume of the papers published in each field, throughout the world, renders it impossible for the typical scientist or technologist to meet his current-awareness need, i.e., to keep abreast of new papers by scanning all the primary publications (periodicals, reports series, etc.) in which they appear. Moreover, he cannot ensure that he has obtained details of all the work already done on a subject by searching a limited number of primary publications. (This latter requirement is frequently termed his information-retrieval need.)

To assist in coping with these problems there have been two main developments. First, information services have been established within the organizations employing scientists and technologists to look after their information needs, namely, notify them of items of interest, collect and organize the primary information so that it is available when they need it, and, if required, search the mass of literature on their behalf. Such information services increased rapidly with the development of the science-based industries. They are now common, at various levels of sophistication, in all government research establishments and technical departments, in research associations (where information services are one of the main services provided to members), and in most industrial and commercial organizations of any importance.

The second development has been that of services seeking to organize the information within a particular discipline or subject field, sometimes on a worldwide basis. Normally all the primary publications produced throughout the world within a subject field or a proportion of them as decided by the publisher will be scanned and their details listed in a periodic publication. Such publications are designated secondary and their contents as secondary information since they contain references to or representations of primary items of information and do not reproduce the items themselves. Although these secondary information services have been produced for many years (e.g., Science Abstracts has been produced by the Institution of Electrical Engineers since 1898), their role has expanded with the massive increase in primary information. They have become one of the main tools of the technical information services serving individual organizations.

In considering the role of secondary information services one must bear in mind the total environment in which they operate. Although there are a very large number of such services operating throughout the world, their influence on the individual scientist or engineer may be less than that of his local technical information service (through whom he normally will receive the products of the secondary service). Although in some organizations the scientist or engineer may receive the secondary publications on circulation from the library or information service for current-awareness scanning, in many organizations the relevant abstracts or titles from these publications are added to the information bulletin issued regularly by the local technical information service. Similarly, although some users conduct their own searches of the literature and thus make use of the abstracts journals and other tools, others have the search carried out on their behalf by the information staff (i.e., as a local enquiry-answering service) and therefore have less contact with the secondary information services used in the search.

The products of the total secondary information service may be conveniently divided into four main classes: abstracts journals, titles listings, SDI (selective dissemination of information) services, and enquiry-answering services. Abstracts journals provide listings with the following features: the title of the document, the author or authors, the bibliographic reference, and an abstract (that is, a brief objective condensation or summary of the document). The items are normally arranged in the abstracts journal by subject or by periodical title and series. Author, subject, and other indexes may be provided either in each issue of the journal or in periodic cumulations. An abstracts journal may thus be used for current awareness by scanning the individual issues, or for retrospective searching by means of its indexes and its classified arrangement. Titles listings normally are produced for current-awareness purposes and are seldom indexed. Apart from abstracts, they normally contain the same elements as the items in abstracts journals.

SDI, or selective dissemination of information, is a system, either manual or computer-based, by which those publications that are likely to be of interest are selected for an individual from the mass of publications produced. In the manual system this is done by information workers who scan the incoming literature and are aware of the information requirements of those individuals who are to be served. In a computer-based system the requirements of each individual are "indexed" to form a profile: these profiles are then compared with the indexing of the documents entering the system and, where the match is sufficient, details of the document are sent to the individual possessing the matching profile. If the individual returns an assessment of the relevance to his interests of the notifications sent to him, his profile may be modified to reflect his requirements more accurately. A variation on this SDI service tailored to the requirements of an individual is the standard-profile SDI service in which a profile is established to cover a stated subject, aspect, or facet, and any number of subscribers may receive the output.

Enquiry-answering services are also commonly referred to as information retrieval or retrospective searching services. In these the published (and often the semipublished) literature is searched in response to a specific enquiry in order to obtain documents that deal with the subject of the enquiry or a piece of information that provides the answer to the enquiry. In the latter instance the answer may be augmented or entirely provided by a specialist in the subject from his own knowledge; such a service is frequently provided by research associations. However, the provision of a list of references is probably the more usual method of enquiry answering by information services and libraries. The references are obtained normally by searches of either the catalogues and indexes compiled by the local information service or abstracts journals, titles lists, and bibliographies produced by the secondary information services.

This discussion has centered mainly around published information such as periodical articles, conference proceedings, and patents and semipublished material such as theses, dissertations, and technical and research reports. Similarly it has been confined to the formal or institutional information network represented by libraries, information centers, and secondary information services. In addition to this formal network, there is an extremely important informal system for the transmission of information. This is conducted mainly on a personal basis, either with colleagues in the organization or with those working in the same field, through correspondence or at conferences and meetings. A large proportion of the information transmitted in this informal way is either verbal or in manuscript or consists of unpublished reports, copies of papers that are to be published subsequently, etc.

In addition to this informal system there is a specialized system dealing with trade or manufacturer's literature, that is, advertisements, handbooks, catalogs, specifications of equipment, components, and materials available. This has its own specialist secondary information services but it is mainly transmitted by periodicals (including free controlled-circulation publications) and by direct mailing by the manufacturers.

Neither the informal systems nor unpublished material nor trade literature was investigated in detail in the present study, although the relative importance to the research worker of these alternative sources of information was studied.

It may be useful to provide an indication of the quantitative importance of the nonprimary information field. Our studies indicate that total expenditure of secondary information services in the United Kingdom may be about £5 million per annum.* Expenditure of technical information services may be approximately £15 million. These figures refer to 1969. Expenditure for the total secondary information services in all the OECD countries may have been about £400 million in 1970.

The introduction of mechanized and computerized systems of secondary information appears likely to raise the costs of secondary information services in the fields affected to some multiple of their present level. On the other hand, these increases in expenditure may have as an offset the reduction of expenditure in the much more extensive field of technical information services within government and industrial firms. And they may also result in savings through the closing down of a number of national secondary information services. This question of the true social costs of the substitution of advanced computerized information systems for more conventional systems is of practical importance. The present study, however, does not focus

---

* £1. = $2.50 at time of writing.

upon this issue, although some of its results indirectly do throw some light upon the question.

An important aspect of the provision of total secondary information systems is that a large part of it is shielded from market forces. If this were not so there might be less need for cost-benefit and cost-effectiveness studies. For in a market environment the supply and price of secondary information services would be governed by the familiar competitive process. In certain restricted and hypothetical conditions (involving perfect competition and freedom from external effects) the volume, quality, and intensity of secondary information services would then be determined by that price which would yield a normal profit in the market.

What are the forces that have caused the provision of total secondary information services to come largely into nonprivate hands? Partly these forces are historical: the information field has to some extent developed out of the public library service. The existence of free information provision in some areas and the constant growth of the scope of such provision must necessarily cause any private entrepreneur to hesitate before lauching an information agency.

Private enterprise does, however, play a role in the provision of total secondary information services. In a few fields companies have emerged that provide information services to private firms at fees that enable the information agencies involved to make a profit. An example of this is the Scientific Documentation Centre in Dunfermline, Scotland. Even in such cases it is doubtful, however, whether any approximation exists to the economist's notion of perfect competition.

An example of the role of competition in the information field sometimes arises from the practice among large firms of providing for their own employees certain tailor-made information services such as selective dissemination services. Some large firms provide such services only in cases where costs are lower than the cost of "buying in" the service from outside; but confidentiality often creates an obstacle to such buying in and efficiency remains a serious problem.

Information is an intangible commodity. In this it differs from goods like coal or wheat. Moreover, it is not used up in the process of consumption, so that unlike electricity, it can be passed from hand to hand without necessarily diminishing in value. Property in intangible commodities is to some degree protected by the patent and copyright laws; but there is probably little legal protection possible for such information services as information retrieval systems. A somewhat similar problem arises—although on a larger scale—with respect to computer programs. These are valuable intellectual artifacts but it is difficult to police any kind of protection for them. A measure of protection is afforded by the fact that some programs are more or less specific to a particular piece of computer hardware. In the case of some information systems the main instrument for ensuring against fee evasion is simply the time and trouble involved in evasion. To a lesser extent, the possible odium of discovery may be a factor. But the possibility of avoidance or evasion of fees sets an upper limit to the fees that can be charged and thus encourages the movement toward public free provision.

It is appropriate to consider to what extent it is wise and sensible that an element of subsidy should be provided to information services. The criteria to be considered are the orthodox economic ones of external economies, decreasing costs, and the speed of transmission of technological innovation.

It is possible that information agencies may operate under conditions of increasing returns, that is, of falling average costs of production. The evidence on this is somewhat inconclusive, and cross-section studies discussed later in this volume provide some apparently contrary evidence. But many of the processes performed by an information agency will have to be duplicated by a second agency operating in the same field, and this suggests that the introduction of competition might raise total costs.

It is normally agreed among economists that a situation with falling average costs of production and consequently with marginal costs below average costs requires some degree of subsidy to achieve optimal output. (The exceptions to this rule involve even greater degrees of falling costs in other sectors, or supply prices of factors very sensitive to the level of output.) Insofar as information agencies are characterized by falling average costs, there is a case for subsidy. The numerical value of such subsidy requires special determination in each particular case.

External effects may require some degree of subsidy as well. Such external effects may arise in information work either because information is passed from hand to hand so that fees are difficult to collect, or it may arise because the technological advances that are made easier by an information system are themselves relatively easy to copy and are insufficiently protected by patents. In either case the net benefits from the existence of an information system may be greater than is indicated by the fees collectable and some degree of subsidy may be appropriate.

The benefits of a private firm's own information system may not, moreover, accrue entirely to the firm utilizing the system. An information system may advance the professional career of the firm's employees and this advance may not accrue to the benefit of the firm involved. The educational value of the information system or the greater professional recognition of the scientist whose work is more successful because of the information system may accrue to the employees through improved bargaining positions and improved wages. To some degree this may be offset by the gain to the firm by virtue of the lag of professional reputation behind actual worth or because employees may be prepared to work for less in an environment in which their education is promoted. But there is certainly no guarantee of perfect harmony.

Not all entrepreneurs or all firms are quick to seize opportunities of profitable innovation. All managers value a quiet life to some degree, and many small firms are particularly slothful. This might not be socially important if it were only the directors and shareholders who suffered; in fact, however, the labor and product markets are imperfect and some of the loss is borne by employees and by customers. It follows, therefore, that any device that can speed the adoption of economically more advanced techniques will have benefits beyond the confines of the firm itself. This is perhaps the strongest reason for a subsidy to information services; without such a subsidy some smaller firms may be inclined to do without the service, to lag technically even more than they would have done, and to pass on some of the loss to employees and customers.

While all these arguments provide some case (necessarily unquantified) for a subsidy to information services, they must be set against the obvious disadvantages, from the point of view of efficiency, of the existence of a subsidy, especially if it is thought likely that the subsidy will be increased if losses occur.

We come now to the question of the international provision of secondary information services. This is perhaps the fastest-growing and certainly the most dramatic section of the market, coupled as it is with complex cataloging and retrieval systems. The forces making for the internationalization of secondary information services are essentially the same as the putative forces making for monopoly in the secondary information service of a single industry or profession in a single country. Briefly these forces are the savings available from performing secondary information activities on the same body of material for the same body of customers in a single agency. In the case of international cooperation, decreasing costs appear especially important because of the heavy initial costs of programming and storing information in computers.

But the introduction of large fixed-cost elements in production will not be worthwhile unless the extent of the market covered is increased. Thus the introduction of computerized secondary information systems leads to pressure for a wider and international market and to pressure for the elimination of competitive national agencies. These developments in the secondary information field offer obvious advantages for the computer-producing industries and the computer-producing countries. The advantages may be somewhat less marked elsewhere. The internationalization of secondary information services opens up problems of fee setting and cost sharing. It is not easy to generalize about the basis of fees and cost sharing in international secondary information services. To some degree this will remain the outcome of international bargaining. One possible system, however, involves the cost contribution of any particular country being confined to a commitment to process information generated in that country. Such a system involves a charge on production of primary information. Insofar as production and use of primary scientific information is perfectly correlated this seems fair. But it is arguable that the basic costs of the international facility should be borne by the largest information user, with only incremental costs being borne by other countries. There is in fact probably no simple system of fees and costs that will be thought "fair" by everyone concerned. The scope for bargaining is certainly considerable, but the net effect of internationalization is likely to be an increase in the average degree of subsidization of information services, together with a considerable transfer of resources from the United States to other countries, at least in the first instance.

From the practical point of view it may be that the most important economic issues in the secondary information field in the next decade will be the extent to which European countries should contribute to the accelerated development of international systems even at the expense of increased secondary information budgets or the running down of their own national secondary information agencies. The subject is a complex one and the present study can throw only incidental light upon it. But one important element in the problem is the extent to which the characteristics of the services provided by international agencies conform to those most desired by national R & D workers. Some useful light is thrown on that subject in the present study. There is limited value in providing secondary information services of great technical capacity if the particular characteristics of the services they offer are not much appreciated by those who use them and if the services they displace offer characteristics more strikingly appreciated.

CHAPTER 2

THEORY

We must now turn to a consideration of the main theoretical and methodological assumptions underlying the present study. It is a commonplace of quantitative work in economics that economic data can seldom be accepted at face value. Statistical data in economics requires a theoretical interpretation. This is the foundation stone of the econometric method. It applies with as much force to the present study as to the traditional problem of the estimation of supply and demand curves.

The present study is based upon the assumption of the existence of a stochastic production function of research output. One of the arguments of this function is the volume of information reaching the research-conducting scientists. Thus we assume the existence of a research production function having the form

$$R = f(S,I)$$
$$S = E + N$$

where R = research output
 S = scientific input
 I = secondary information input
 N = information activity among scientific personnel
 E = scientific research activity of such personnel

We assume that an increase in I will increase R if S is constant—i.e., $\partial R / \partial I > 0$,—by reducing N-activities and increasing E-activities among scientists. We do not deal with the possibility that an increase in I will reduce the efficiency of E-activities by causing a diversion of E-effort into wasteful reading activities. We assume that scientists will optimize their reading activities and will not read more than is necessary, regardless of the secondary information flow. If this assumption were violated so that an increase in the secondary information available to scientists caused them to divert their efforts into unproductive lines of study the conclusions of our work would have to be modified. Put symbolically, this assumption may be expressed thus:

$$R = f(S, I)$$
$$S = E + N$$
$$E = g(Q, T)$$
$$Q = Q(I)$$

Here T is the number of hours of scientific effort devoted to scientific work and Q is the "quality" of these hours. We assume that $Q = Q(I)$, and that $dQ/dI \geq 0$. Further, our main calculations are based on the assumptions that

$$N = N(I)$$
$$E = E(I)$$

and that

$$\frac{dN}{dI} < 0$$
$$\frac{dE}{dI} > 0$$

Briefly this says that the amount of information work performed by scientists depends upon the secondary information services available and that an increase in secondary information services available will reduce the amount of information-type activities performed by scientists. Furthermore, these relationships indicate that the volume of scientific research activity increases with the volume of secondary information supplied to the research personnel.

There are certain psychological assumptions upon which our calculations also depend. We assume in particular that the amount of research output depends in a proportional fashion upon the number of hours of research effort undertaken by each scientific worker. There is no evidence offered for this proposition and if some other relationship—say a logarithmic one—prevailed, our numerical results would be affected. The testing of this assumption is, however, rather beyond the scope of economic study and lies in the field of psychology.

A further notable characteristic of this study is its acceptance of the information user's satisfaction as the proper basis of benefit evaluation. Again there is the acceptance of the existing salary structure as a measure of the research worker's research productivity. These assumptions naturally affect the quantitative results or this study. If, for example, it should be desired to test the implications of the proposition that younger research workers are underpaid in terms of their productivity, while older workers are overpaid, an adjustment in terms of a "shadow wage" based on age is possible within the terms of this study.

One characteristic of this study that will be specially noted by economists is that cost-effectiveness measures are calculated on the basis of total provision rather than on the basis of incremental provision. This is made necessary by the fact that the provision of particular sorts of secondary information does not have any clearly defined quantitative measure. It is not possible to think in terms of varying the quantity of abstracts available. The situation must be considered in terms of full provision or no provision. The method principally adopted is most easily conceived as answering questions about the desirability of continuing a particular service.

Our procedure in this study is to value each particular information service separately and to arrive at total values to the firm and the economy by amalgamating these individual values. This procedure depends upon the assumption that relations of substitutability and complementarity between services are not very great and that the degree of commercial competition between establishments engaging in research and development is not excessive. Our method could be modified to relax those assumptions if this were thought necessary. Such an alteration would reduce somewhat the values attached to information services as a whole.

A further aspect of the present study is that, wherever possible, alternative measures of cost-effectiveness are derived on the basis of alternative assumptions. One of the merits of this approach is that it is possible to examine the sensitivity of results to the choice of assumptions made, and this is done wherever possible.

Economists have in the past been reluctant to rely upon surveys of consumers' expressed preferences. They have mainly inclined to the view that only choice revealed in the market could offer evidence about consumers' underlying preferences. This self-denying ordinance has not prevented economists from developing exceedingly useful theoretical structures of demand analysis. Nevertheless, it has resulted in the neglect of a rich source of data, which has in fact been exploited largely by psychologists and marketing specialists. An essential feature of the present study is its attempt to utilize questionnaire techniques to evaluate the benefits of certain economic activities. Some economists will reject this "attitudinal" approach out of hand; others will accept that the validity of the approach must depend upon the predictive success of the method. The present study does not lend itself to predictive test, however, and the reader must be referred to the extensive marketing literature for analysis of the problems involved and the success of the general approach.

Our study provides an opportunity for examining the extent to which simple and readily available measures, like those derived from questioning information officers, will provide good proxies for measures derived from more complex, time consuming, and expensive procedures.

The primary aim of this study is to develop a methodology for the evaluation of cost effectiveness issues in secondary information. The development of quantitative measures has been only of secondary interest. The relatively narrow coverage and restricted sample utilized limit the reliance that can be placed upon the figures generated. It may be hoped that later studies will increase the scope and accuracy of the results.

Several different measures of effectiveness were derived with the objective of providing alternative methods of measuring the same thing and these should in principle give similar answers. The first, and basic, measure of effectiveness is the value of the time saved by the R & D worker in using secondary information services. This measure is based upon the assumption that the user of information would have to increase the amount of time spent searching for and reading information if secondary information services were not available to him, and would accordingly reduce the time spent actually performing his R & D activities; the underlying assumption is that there is a linear relationship between the output of R & D workers and the time they spend on this activity.

An alternative measure, which takes account of the possibility of a nonlinear relationship between time and output, is the value of the time required by the R & D worker to achieve his former level of output were he deprived of secondary information. These two measures are alternative methods of expressing the value of secondary information services to the firm, but they take no account of the value of the services to the individual himself.

This individual value was defined as being the increase in salary the individual would require if he were deprived of access to secondary information services, and the problem here is that this value may or may not overlap with either of the previous two measures. A sensitivity analysis was adopted whereby these measures were combined in various proportions to assess whether or not overlap would make any difference to the results.

A further measure of the value was to ask the individual to assess the degree of his dependence on secondary information on an arbitrary scale; this dependence index was then weighted in various ways to make it consistent with the previous measures. The comparison of the outcome of these different measures provides a basis for testing the effectiveness methodology. The cost measures that were devised were the total identifiable costs of each information system, and these costs were split between the different services where possible.

The effectiveness and cost measures were then brought together into a single cost-effectiveness relationship wherever possible. Thus comparisons could be made between different services and between different types of service. Some progress was also made in determining which of the characteristics of the information services contributed most to the total effectiveness of the particular service. This may be of importance when decisions are taken on the establishment of a new service.

THE NATURE OF COST-BENEFIT ANALYSIS

This section is intended to provide a survey of some of the theoretical issues raised in this study. To some degree these theoretical problems remain unsolved. In practice it was not always possible to conduct the study in a way that would meet all the theoretical objectives. Sometimes a theoretically desirable measurement has not proved to be practicable. Such shortcuts and evasions are by no means unusual in practical economic studies.

Cost-benefit analysis is the construction of a decision-making rule. It is an attempt to measure the net effects of an investment project or other activity on output or welfare and to place the evaluation of projects in the nonmarket sector on a par with the evaluation of projects in a perfectly operating market sector. Cost-benefit analysis and its modification (cost-effectiveness analysis and performance and program budgeting) were developed in, and their primary application has been to, the public sector, but they are equally applicable to intrafirm decisions concerning the efficiency of projects, programs, and departments that are not subject to a direct market test. They have been applied to transportation,[1] education,[2] retraining the unemployed,[3] water resource development,[4] national defense,[5] urban development programs,[6] and many other things.[7] They can be applied to information systems and services as well.

Cost-benefit is a generic term and there are several versions of it. It can be used to decide the cheapest way of achieving some given objective. This is called cost-effectiveness analysis. Cost-effectiveness is a version of cost-benefit that is necessary when benefits cannot be measured in value terms. It measures the costs of alternative means of achieving some defined objective.

The common thread in these alternative but not basically different applications of cost-benefit analysis is the question of efficiency.

They are concerned with maximizing social output per unit of input, that is, imposing the same efficiency criteria on the public or non-market sector that a perfectly competitive price system is said to impose on the private market sector. In the public or other nonmarket sector, if the benefits from a project exceed its costs, both properly discounted—or as it is usually stated, if the cost-benefit ratio exceeds unity—the project is deemed worthwhile. In the private sector, if the internal rate of return exceeds the opportunity cost of capital (the interest rate) the project is profitable and thus worthwhile. These two criteria are in some important respects identical. The superficial difference is that the private firm is comparing rates or ratios of income flows; whereas cost-benefit analysis is a comparison of present values. This can readily be seen as follows. The internal rate of return to a firm arising from a project can be computed by solving the following formula for r:

$$\sum_t E_t (1+r)^{-t} = \sum_t R_t (1+r)^{-t} \qquad (1)$$

where r = the internal rate of return (or marginal efficiency of capital)
E_t = the costs or expenditure on the project in year t
R_t = gross returns (or benefits) in year t

The internal rate of return, r, is the rate of discount that equates the present value of the future returns of an investment with the present value of the costs. Insofar as r exceeds the opportunity cost of capital (the interest rate) to the firm, the investment is profitable and a profit-maximizing firm will accept all projects where this condition prevails.

The cost-benefit ratio can be defined as follows:

$$B/C = \frac{\sum_t R_r (1+i)^{-t}}{\sum_t E_t (1+i)^{-t}} \qquad (2)$$

where i is the interest rate or opportunity cost of capital.* The numerator is the present value of all benefits arising from the project; the denominator the present value of costs.

---

*The interest rate and the opportunity cost of capital may not be the same thing insofar as there are costs other than interest involved in the raising of new capital or if capital rationing exists so that the acquisition of new capital restricts the ability or increases the cost to firms of acquiring capital in the future.

The formula for the internal rate of return (1) can alternatively be written:

$$1.0 = \frac{\sum_t R_t(1+r)^{-t}}{\sum_t E_t(1+r)^{-t}} \quad (3)$$

If $i = r$, equations (2) and (3) are identical. Computing the internal rate of return is equivalent to computing the rate of discount that makes the benefit-cost ratio equal to unity. If the benefit-cost ratio is greater than unity, it follows that r is greater than i, and vice versa. The two decision-making criteria are the same.

Figure 2.1 illustrates a hypothetical evaluation of an information service costing £1,000 per year. Gross annual benefits equal the area oabc or (1.2) x (£1,000) = £1,200; gross annual costs equal the area oade or (1.0) x (£1,000) = £1,000; the cost benefit ratio is 1.2; and the investment in the information service is thus worthwhile.

Rather than evaluating projects on the basis of the cost-benefit ratio or internal rate of return, an alternative measure of efficiency is to rank or otherwise assess projects on the basis of net benefits,

FIGURE 2.1

Hypothetical Evaluation of an Information Service

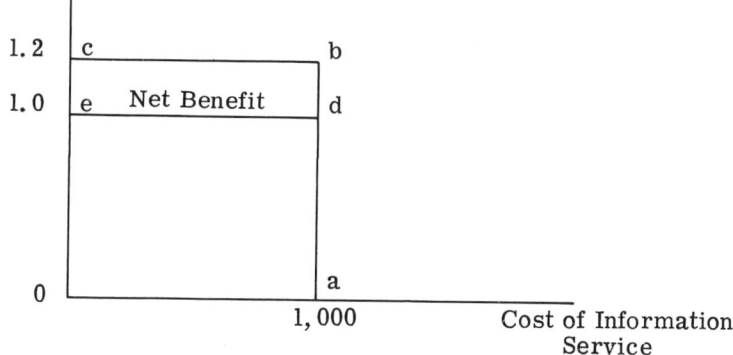

Source: Compiled by the authors.

that is, gross benefits minus gross costs or area edbc.* Evaluating projects on the basis of net benefits is equivalent to the ratio or rate-of-return methods in that all three discriminate consistently between "profitable" and "unprofitable" projects. If the cost-benefit ratio is greater than unity, net benefits must be positive, and as noted above, the internal rate of return must exceed the interest rate. If a project is "profitable" (unprofitable) according to one criterion, it must be "profitable" (unprofitable) according to the others as well. However, with respect to relative rankings of projects all of which are "profitable," the rankings may differ depending on which criterion is employed.

INTERNAL VERSUS EXTERNAL COSTS AND BENEFITS

A distinguishing factor between profit maximization in the private sector and welfare maximization in the public sector is the inclusion of externalities in the decision-making criterion of the latter.† Profit maximizing firms will consider only the returns and costs borne by them, whereas welfare maximizing public decisions must include in the decision calculus the external or spill-over benefits and costs that accrue to other parties. Thus, with respect to a cost-effectiveness or benefit evaluation of an activity within society or a firm, such as the use of an information service, two alternative evaluations are possible. One includes only those returns and costs that accrue to the firm, thus evaluating the activity with respect to the profitability of the firm. The other includes the external benefits and costs borne by other units within the private sector or by government, thus evaluating the activity with respect to global efficiency or the allocation of resources within society.

ESTIMATING BENEFITS

The simplest manufactured component involved in push-button warfare is the push button. The formula of the cost-benefit ratio offered above is the push button of cost-benefit analysis. In order to implement the analysis, the difficult task of estimating the costs and

---

*Still another measure is to convert the flows of benefits and costs into annuity streams.

†Some qualification of this dogmatic assertion of the identity of perfect competitive outcomes with cost-benefit choices may be necessary.

benefits must be undertaken. To a very large extent the specific methodology of benefit and cost estimation is unique to the specific project or activity under investigation.

The first task in evaluating a project is to estimate area oabc in Figure 2.1, the gross benefits. There are various ways to do this. Basically, what one wishes to know is: what is the value of the increased welfare that results from the project, or equivalently, how much would the recipients of the benefits be willing to pay rather than forego the consumption of these benefits? One possible way of estimating these benefits is to obtain the opinion of responsible administrators. In this study the research director or budget allocator and the information officer or librarian of each firm were asked: "If the annual purchase price for some element of the services were to rise, at what price level would the establishment stop subscribing to it?" The question, in effect, asks these persons to do the benefit analysis, to assess the value of the service to the firm in terms of the maximum amount the firm would be willing to pay for it. The assessments by these individuals constitute independent estimates of gross benefits and may be used as checks against alternative estimates. The answers solicited presumably refer to benefits over and above the cost of using the information service inside the firm. Thus by this approach gross benefits are the maximum amount the administrators of firms would be willing to pay producers of the service plus the cost of utilizing the service within the firm.

Ignoring internal costs in the computation of both benefits and costs would, since they constitute a constant in both the numerator and denominator of a time cost-benefit ratio, tend to lower any ratios above unity and raise any ratios below unity but leave relative ratings unchanged. On the other hand, neglecting them would have no effect on the calculation of net benefits alone because in this case they cancel out.

Another route to the estimation of benefits might be to compute the opportunity cost of *not* using the information service. One might compute the cost of achieving the same level of effectiveness or benefit through the cheapest alternative means. If the cost of producing the same benefit by alternative means is greater than the cost of the information service, the information service is cost effective. When employing and interpreting the alternative cost approach to the estimation of gross benefits, the alternative that is costed must be the best alternative. This is to say that in the absence of the option of an information service, the alternative strictly must have a cost-benefit ratio greater than unity in its own right. Otherwise it is an irrelevant alternative and its cost does not necessarily reflect the opportunity cost of not using an information service.

Two alternative methods of making this calculation may be considered. In each evaluation the lower cost alternative ought properly to be selected as the measure of the benefits (that is, cost savings) of an information service. In the first method the firm would duplicate the information services to its researchers itself. Consider the answers to the question: "What would the cost to the establishment be if it had to provide all the secondary information used within each establishment from each of the following external services?" Another estimate is implicit in the cost data provided by the information services. Assuming that the firm could produce the product as effectively as the information service, the cost to a firm of providing the service for itself is the total fixed cost of the information service plus the variable cost associated with providing the service to a single subscriber. (Because only a small percentage of the information services used by firms were costed, this second alternative could not be utilized in the present study.)

A different opportunity cost measure might be derived by considering what would happen within the firm in the absence of an information service. Researchers would presumably spend more time retrieving information from primary sources. The increased time required to gather this information represents a loss to the firm.

Thus the cost of this alternative is the increased time researchers spend retrieving information from primary sources, and, on the assumption that workers are paid according to their marginal productivity, the cost to the firm is this increase in time spent retrieving information times the wage rate of these workers. The saving of these costs represents the benefit of an information system.

This alternative may impose still other costs on a firm. If increased reliance is placed on primary information sources, more of them may be required; the saving of these costs must be included as part of the benefits of an information service as well. There are, however, several alternative ways in which adjustment could be made and these ought properly to be considered. These possible alternative adjustments include an increase in the total time spent on research. But an increase in time spent on primary literature might imply a reduction of other activities of R & D workers. It may mean a reduction of the time spent on administration or other activities by part-time research workers. It may mean an increase in the total time spent by R & D workers on the activities associated with their job, whether these activities be conducted in the laboratory, the office, or at home. In each case there will be a change in behavior pattern, and these changes could in principle be measured and costed. Each such measure is likely to give a different valuation.

It should be noted that although this discussion refers to the "benefits to the firm," it is by no means certain that the firm or its owners are the ultimate recipients of these benefits. The price system will distribute them throughout society. For example, if firms sell in competitive markets and information services yield a positive net benefit or cost saving and all firms use them, the cost saving will at least in part be passed on to the consumer in lower prices. It is necessary in principle to evaluate the benefits at the source before they are reflected in prices and distributed throughout the system. The method employed in this study attempts to do this. One possible exception may be the use of the wage rate to evaluate the time cost of spending more time on primary sources. This study involves an expost evaluation, and insofar as information services yield a net benefit by raising the marginal productivity of research and development labor, this already may be reflected in the wage. This only applies to the market as a whole. No bias is present with respect to the estimation of benefits accruing to an individual firm insofar as the wage is market determined.

EXTERNAL BENEFITS

There are benefits that may accrue to parties other than the owners of the firm from an information system. One is not concerned here with those benefits that are later shifted by price effects. These are included in the above estimates of internal benefits. Rather, the issue is whether or not there are direct spill-over effects on other parties arising from the adoption of an information service. The most significant spill-over would seem to be the benefits that accrue to workers in better job amenities. In this study research workers were asked: "How great an increase in salary would you require to take an otherwise identical job in a firm that did not carry any information services?" Assuming their responses are accurate these assessments are the external benefits to workers. (Just as the benefit of an information service to a firm takes the form of increasing the productivity and demand for the research and development labor, the creation of job amenities increases the supply.)

THE WESSEL AND MOORE REPORT

Before going on to give a brief summary of the main findings of the present investigation, it may be useful to provide here a brief synopsis of the main points emerging from the recently compiled study of library services by C. S. Wessel and K. L. Moore, prepared for the U.S. government.[8]

The study is, as far as we are aware, the main alternative economic investigation of cost-effectiveness in the information field currently available. It provides, among other things, an excellent and comprehensive literature survey. The existence of this report and of the survey it contains should certainly be noted by those interested in the present volume.

It would be an unnecessary duplication of effort for us to resurvey the literature covered in the Wessel and Moore report. We have nothing significant to add to their comments.* The report is in essence an application of cost-effectiveness techniques to library functions; it is, broadly speaking, attempting to attain the same objectives as the present study in a different field of information dissemination and it is worthwhile to concentrate some discussion on the ways in which our approach compares with it.

The report is in three parts, the first of which is a review of the state theory in this and related fields; this review is impressive in its scope and appears to cover everything that had been written on the subject up to the date of writing. The second part of the report is concerned with evaluating the various criteria that could be used to assess effectiveness and with collecting data. The third part sets out the recommended criteria and the methods for their utilization; we shall be concerned here almost exclusively with the third part.

There are four basic methods of approach, some of which are more or less complementary to one another, and the acronyms with the accompanying key phrases are as follows:

1. Score analysis: Service components reliability and efficiency analysis
2. Scout analysis: Service components utility analysis
3. Core analysis: Correlation, regression and effectiveness analysis
4. Game analysis: Group attainment and method analysis

Each of these methods of approach will now be examined in turn.

Score Analysis

This analysis adopts a probabilistic approach to the number of needs met based on sample data collected within the library and does

---

*However, special mention must be made of the useful work of J. Hagwood and W. Morely, of Durham University, who undertook a utility-based survey of information needs in the Durham libraries: P.E.B.U.L. Report: Project for Evaluating Benefits from University Library Durham University, O.S.T.I. Report No. 5056, October 1969. Their approach has certain similarities to our own.

not make any allowance for the utility values to the user of these needs. The measure of effectiveness is defined as the probability of meeting the requirement of any need, and the approach concentrates on the variation in this probability that results from adopting new procedures or methods of meeting the need and relates this to cost. The difference between the probabilities of success of two courses of action is calculated, and the difference in unit cost is also computed to give what is called the "delta index of effectiveness"

$$\frac{\Delta E}{\Delta C}$$

where ΔE = the difference in the probability of success of two methods of approach
ΔC = the difference in their unit cost.

Thus if some addition to the present service is planned in a library then that addition which gives the highest delta index of effectiveness will be undertaken.

There is no reason why this approach could not be extended to certain aspects of information systems, but as the number of needs met was not one of our measures of effectiveness there is no parallel to this approach in this study.

Scout Analysis

In this case the utility of a service is related to its cost and this approach bears the most similarity to our own of the four methods employed.

The utility value of a service is estimated by the librarian and is based on (a) the kinds and degrees of each service and product given; and (b) the effect of the information derived from the respective service or product in meeting a specific within mission need or in leading the user to a potential approach for meeting his within mission goals.[9]

The different services are ranked in order of importance by the librarian and a cardinal utility measure is placed on each; for example if there are three services then the one in the middle of the ranking is given an index or 10 and the others are weighted in relation to this. This value—in terms of "utils"—is then multiplied by the number of needs to give a base measure of value for each service. It is acknowledged in the report that this method of procedure lacks credibility because it was found that different librarians gave different utility measures to the same services; it was found that the individual librarian's judgment on utility is usually consistent with his judgments on how funds should be allocated. In this context the correlation between the information officer's estimate and the calculated values of effectiveness in Chapter 4 should be noted.

The process of assigning a utility value to the services produced is somewhat similar to the concept of our effectiveness measures; however, the method of calculation is rather different. In our case the information officer was asked to place a monetary value on the information services used in whatever way he saw fit, while the librarian in the Wessel and Moore report is given a restricted basis from which to operate. One advantage of the Wessel and Moore method is that the criteria they place before the librarian are those that have been agreed on by a large number of librarians and thus may lead to a greater degree of consistency than that achieved in our report. However, it was not our intention to use the information officer's estimate of value as an operational effectiveness measure unless it could be demonstrated that it agreed very closely with the values placed on the services by the users; we have made the assumption that the user is best qualified to make judgments on the value of information services and this is the essential point of difference in the two methods of approach.

The Wessel and Moore method then proceeds with an examination of the effect on utility of varying the input in the various services in isolation; the input can be varied either by (a) increasing or decreasing the number of needs met, or (b) increasing or decreasing the standard of the service provided and hence the utility of the needs met.

This requires a series of additional arbitrary value judgments on the part of the librarian. A total utility schedule is then constructed for each type of service, and from this schedule the marginal utility of a given variation in the service is computed and the cost of this variation in output is computed from the cost-accounting data. Once this procedure has been carried out for each service the library produces, then the marginal utility of each can be related to the cost of each and this provides a basis for examining the allocation of funds on the principle that the ratio of marginal utility to cost should be equal in all lines to achieve optimal allocation. Thus funds can be directed from services with a low ratio to those with a high ratio, subject to the reservation that this does not conflict with long-run policy requirements and other wider considerations.

At this stage it is difficult to see how this optimization approach could be usefully applied to information systems, particularly given the rather dubious nature of the marginal utility calculations.

Core Analysis

This approach is concerned with establishing an empirical basis for evaluating the amount of work done in relation to the input and examines the correlation between costs and outputs. The example given is the cost of cataloging. It was found that no relationship existed between the total cost of cataloging and the number of items processed when examining a cross-section of libraries, but when the cataloging activity had been broken down by quality, judged on the basis of the use of specialized subject terms, a correlation of .95 was obtained between costs and output. This result compares with the correlation of .938 obtained in Chapter 4 ("The Cost of an Abstract") of this report, where the cost per abstract is correlated with an index of quality. (A similar result might also be obtained if the unit cost of cataloging were correlated with an index of quality of the cataloged items; however, this operation was not carried out by Wessel and Moore.)

Using the least-squares techniques, Wessel and Moore compute a line of best fit for the libraries in each quality class, and this is used as a quality control measure in that any libraries that do not lie close to the line are subjected to examination. It can be noted that there is no evaluation of the internal procedures of any library required here.

Game Analysis

This is the application of work study methods to the production of library services; this adopts a purely operational approach and does not compare with our method.

NOTES

1. M. E. Beesley and C. D. Foster, "The Victoria Line: Social Benefits and Finances," Journal of the Royal Statistical Society 128, part 1 (1965); H, Nohring and M. Harwitz, Highway Benefits: An Analytical Approach (Evanston, Ill.: Northwestern University Press, 1962); D. M. Winch, The Economics of Highway Planning (Toronto: University of Toronto Press, 1963).

2. M. Blaug, "The Rate of Return on Investment in Education in Great Britain," The Manchester School 33, no. 3 (September 1965); W. L. Hansen, "Total and Private Rates of Return to Investment in Schooling," Journal of Political Economy 21 (April 1963).

3. M. E. Borus, "A Benefit Cost Analysis of the Economic Effectiveness of Retraining the Unemployed," Yale Economic Essays 4, no. 2 (Fall 1964).

4. J. V. Krutilla and Otta Eckstein, Multiple Purpose River Development (Baltimore: Johns Hopkins University Press, 1958); J. Hirschleifer, J. C. de Haven, and J. W. Williams, Water Supply,

Economics, Technology and Policy (Chicago: University of Chicago Press, 1960).

5. G. J. Mitch and R. N. McKean, The Economics of Defence in the Nuclear Age (London: Oxford University Press, 1960); R. N. McKean, Efficiency in Government through Systems Analysis (New York: John Wiley, 1958).

6. Jerome Rothenberg, Economic Evaluation of Urban Renewal (Washington: The Brookings Institution, 1967); N. Lichfield, Cost Benefit Analysis in Urban Redevelopment, Research Report, Real Estate Research Program, Institute of Business and Economic Research (Berkeley: University of California, 1962).

7. For excellent surveys of cost-benefit methodology, see A. R. Prest and R. Turvey, "Cost Benefit Analysis," Economic Journal, December 1965; and D. Querin, The Capital Expenditure Decision (Homewood, Ill.: Richard D. Irwin, 1967).

8. C. J. Wessel and K. L. Moore, Criteria for Evaluating the Effectiveness of Library Operations and Services Army Technical Library Improvement Studies, Report no. 21 (Washington, D.C., January 1969).

9. Ibid., p. 40.

CHAPTER

3

THE STUDY

In this chapter we will discuss in detail the procedures employed in the study and the way in which they generate the results displayed in Chapter 4. Our procedure will be to examine in turn: grading, characteristics, weighting, sampling, and aggregation. Then we will consider the effectiveness questionnaire, and finally we will discuss the procedures used in costing secondary information services in the study. Some of this is rather arduous reading, and the nonspecialist may find it convenient to skip the latter parts of this chapter until he has had a chance to study the results of the exercise when he may return to the task with a clearer motivation.

As an appendix to Chapter 3 we present some data on the nature of the sample studied. This material is of interest as a rough check on the acceptability of the sample drawn, but it is of some little interest in itself because of the fascination of the information which it seems to reveal about research and development workers. It will, however, be borne in mind that our study is by no means a true sample of the total R & D population, so its results must be treated with proper caution.

GRADING

Grading is the process whereby value is allotted to particular commodities or services; in our case, secondary information.

There are various methods by which this can be achieved, either by the use of "objective" or physical methods or by reliance upon subjective judgments. The latter raises the question of whose subjective judgments to take into consideration and by what means different opinions are to be aggregated. The grading adopted depends partly upon the resources available and partly upon the ease and accuracy with which questions can be comprehended and answered.

Alan Cartter in his article "Economics of the University," written on the basis of a survey done by the American Council for Education (ACE), offers an interesting practical example.1 The article deals with the problem of evaluating quality in graduate education in economics and of judging the effectiveness of doctoral programs and covers many of the problems of grading.

The ACE chose as the basis for the grading of the quality of faculty of the leading American economics departments, a subjective ranking from 1 . . . N, according to the judgments of four different categories of individuals—heads of departments, distinguished senior scholars, junior scholars who had received Ph.D.s not more than ten years before, and a small panel of 13 experts consisting of editors of the major economic journals and others of recognized academic stature. The rankings are stratified four ways by geographical areas.

To provide what Cartter refers to as a "combined score," a separate overall ranking order of quality, the rankings of the different categories are aggregated. This process involves a straightforward addition of the number of firsts, number of seconds . . . number of twentieths, etc., allotted to each university department. No allowance is made for weighting by salary or distinction, thereby equating a first from the expert panel with that of, for example, junior scholars.

The results yield interesting comparisons of the rankings of the differently qualified groups; notably that in the rankings of the first three groups, junior and senior scholars and department heads are closely correlated, while there is a certain variance between these and the rankings of the expert panel. There is also shown to be a slight geographical bias, generally in favor of local universities.

While the author admits some very real limitations to such subjective evaluations—"a compendium of gossip" based only partly on first-hand knowledge influenced by hearsay—it was felt that they rendered a more accurate ranking of quality than alternative "objective" measures, such as the number of research grants obtained, the number of fellows enrolled, or the number of books in the library.

Objective bases for grading are, however, employed for comparison with the subjective ratings and correlation coefficients are calculated between the results obtained by the different methods. The index of quality obtained from the aggregated rankings is compared first with a "scholarly publications" index. The latter is based on a count of all articles, communications, and book reviews appearing in major economic journals, assigning different weights to the various types of publications. This comparison indicates a very close correlation between the quantity of publications and the subjective opinion rankings, for example, the top 25 departments (in the ranking) account for nearly 90 percent of all publications reviewed.

A second comparison yields the conclusion that there is a high correlation between the quality index and the level of faculty salaries. The relationship between average quality ratings and faculty salaries provides a correlation coefficient of 0.872. Thus two "objective" measures seem to support the subjective opinions concerning the quality of economics departments.

A further two "objective" measures of the quality of departments—the annual economic doctorates awarded and the annual doctorates awarded in all subjects—provide a poorer correlation with the "quality index" (for example, six institutions in the top half of the quality index produced less than 10 Ph.D.s in the decade 1953-62, while nine departments with 25 or more doctorates awarded in the decade were on the bottom half of the list). It would be possible to use such physical measures as a proxy for a more time-consuming survey.

This raises the related question of reliance upon a single grading measure, the ranking of an expert as a proxy for all other exercises, as used by Raymond Hughes in his American surveys of 1924 and 1934.[2]

In the present study, as in the ACE survey, subjective values are relied upon for the grading process. The individual R & D workers are required at several instances to give a value to all secondary information, the importance of different characteristics, their satisfaction with and dependence upon information, etc.

No use has been made in this study of physical or "objective" measures as a basis for the grading of secondary information. A possible measure of this type might be a count of the number of references or requests made for primary information by R & D workers as a result of reading the secondary literature. While at first glance this measure would appear to give an accurate evaluation of the effectiveness of secondary information, it could be misleading for a number of reasons. It would be difficult to give an accurate count of the "follow-up" from secondary information. The research worker has several possible sources for this primary information, for example, his own literature, libraries, his firm's library, or a photocopy of the original article or book from the producer of the secondary information in question. While an assessment could be made of the last source, lack of information on the alternatives would render this result an inaccurate measure of the value of the secondary information. Secondly, it is conceivable that the abstract itself may be so comprehensive that it satisfies the need of the information user, precluding the need for a reference to the primary literature. Lastly, the secondary information could be misleading or badly compiled, causing the research worker to apply for primary information that in fact proves useless for his purposes.

The last point concerning the grading process used in this study deals with the use and reliance upon an "expert panel." It is arguable that no panel is more "expert" in the judgment of the effectiveness of secondary information than the information users, the R & D workers. The evaluations of the information officers could be considered the only other "candidates" for such a position, and it is possible that their measures of value be used as a proxy for the other measures. Certainly interesting results may emerge from the comparison of the evaluations of the two groups.

CHARACTERISTICS

It is possible to use the attitudes of information users to develop measures of effectiveness of information services. However, it would be both interesting and valuable to know why, or in what respects, one information service is valued more highly by users than another. An attempt is made in this study to break down the total evaluation of a service's effectiveness into measures that can be attached specifically to the various characteristics of an information system.

A basic problem will be to determine the relative weight to be given to these alternative measures of performance in deciding on the appropriate information package to be chosen to meet a given information need. A further problem is the extent to which the possession of superior performance in one or another characteristic is correlated with a high level of total satisfaction. It is the purpose of the present chapter to explore the notion of alternative measures of performance and to attempt to ascertain the degree to which it can be made into a useful tool of analysis.

We are interested in the behavior of a person seeking a particular type of information and faced with a choice of different information services. The different characteristics of secondary information demanded can be identified conveniently by classifying secondary information by the purpose for which it is required, and by considering the relationship between use and means of supply for each type of information classified. For example, the total demand for information may be split into two divisions: (a) information required for keeping the user up to date in his fields of interest (current awareness need), and (b) information required by the user for a more specific purpose (information retrieval need). It may be necessary to subdivide the latter class into arbitrary sections according to the degree of detail of the information demanded.

The practical steps that might be involved in obtaining numerical characteristics are outlined briefly below.

1. Identification of secondary information services that are used. This could be done simply by surveying the individual information users in the sample population and asking which specific sources of secondary information are used.

2. Identification of the relevant variables in the relationship and their relative importance. It is important to specify the relationship correctly. Two possibilities are available. The sample of information users might be asked which factors influence their choice of information service. Alternatively, each user could be asked to choose from a list of potential influences those of which he is aware. There are a number of weaknesses in the latter approach but it seems that it is more likely to produce results in a form that can be conveniently interpreted and analyzed.

A survey of the literature on information systems provides a useful means by which the potentially important characteristics of information services may be identified. These stem largely from the nature of secondary information services and the functions they are intended to fulfill. A secondary information service is designed to permit an information user to scan and choose items that appear to be of interest to him without the necessity of expending time and effort in looking at all the primary material. The provision of secondary information services thus allows the information user to cover a given number of primary sources in a shorter time interval.

Secondary information services tend to provide material in the form of a list of titles of abstracts that may or may not be classified according to the subject field or may be supplemented by an author or subject index. These potential sources of difference between secondary information services affect the characteristics of the service in which we are interested. They include briefly the speed, or the time delay, in receiving secondary information after the appearance of the corresponding primary material, the relevance of the information supplied to the need, the extent of the coverage of primary information sources, the location of the supply of the service, the degree of detail in the content of the information supplied, and whether the service permits retrieval of secondary information or is designed merely for current use. An example of the latter would be whether or not the service is indexed.

A feature of the characteristics indicated above is that some are complementary while others are competitive in the sense that for a given cost an increase in amount or quality of one characteristic will either contribute to or detract from the value of others. A possible example of this might be, say, a titles list service. If the speed of publication were increased, with constant expenditure on the service, this would tend to reduce the degree of detail or arrangement and indexing if coverage were maintained. Most of the characteristics compete with each other for expenditure resources. The one characteristic that tends to complement others is relevance. If arrangement or indexing were improved, we might expect relevance to increase correspondingly. At the same time, an increase in coverage might result in an increase of irrelevant information.

It seems probable that these characteristics will tend to exert differing degrees of influence on the pattern of use. This will depend partly on the type of need. The sample user might be asked to rank the characteristics that influence his choice of service according to their relative importance. By use of a simple weighting process it should be possible by combining the ranking assigned to each characteristic by the sample population of users for each of the two information needs—current awareness and information retrieval—to ascertain the degree of importance of each characteristic in influencing the demand for any given secondary information service by the given population of information users.

3. Estimation of the quantitative content of the characteristics. There are a number of different methods by which the characteristics might be given numerical content and the choice of any particular one will depend largely on practical considerations. Three possible methods that might be employed are:

(a) Use of each service by a subgroup of the sample of information users. It should be possible to select a subgroup of information users from the total sample of users who identified the determinant characteristics to carry out assessment of the numerical content of these characteristics for the services used by the total sample population. This could be done by stratifying the subgroup by subject field of interest in order to obtain groups of users with similar interests and likely to be faced by the same choice of services, and to obtain a set of estimates of each determinant characteristic for each service. The estimates for each characteristic for a given service could then be summed and averaged, allowing each service to be reflected by a set of measures in respect to each of the determinant characteristics.

(b) Assessment by total sample of information users. This consists of asking each individual in the sample his opinion of the value that should be assigned from the prearranged scale of measurement in respect to each characteristic for the service he uses. If the respondent uses a large number of services, the effort involved might not be acceptable and it might be desirable to limit the number of services to those with which the respondent is most familiar. It should be possible to explain why one service appears to be more effective than another by comparing values for the different characteristics. The more effective service would be expected to possess higher values for the characteristics. Insofar as the two do not correlate, the values of the determinant characteristics will act as a useful means whereby assessments of relative effectiveness may be tested. If a discrepancy arises, the significance of the effectiveness measures may be suspect.

(c) A further use to which the determinant characteristic values might be put would be to investigate the degree to which they explain the demand for a service. By regressing the determinant characteristic values for each service against the values for amount of use or the values for effectiveness of each service, estimates of the ability of the determinant characteristic to explain the pattern would be obtained. Given that a high multiple correlation coefficient is obtained, the estimated values of the coefficients in the relationship would give an indication of the relative importance of each characteristic in determining demand at the margin.

EFFECTIVENESS QUESTIONNAIRE

To ensure a good response rate and the reliability of the response a personal approach was made. The questionnaire is divided into three parts, the first two for officials of the firm—the librarian/information officer and the research director or budget allocator—and the third for R & D workers in the sample.

The information we wish to obtain concerns the ability of different types of secondary information services to satisfy the information needs of the users. We require measures of satisfaction or effectiveness for the different types of service, and the questions thus fall into two main categories: (a) questions eliciting raw measures of relative effectiveness, and (b) questions whose answers will allow refinement, classification, and comparison of the raw data. A third category elicits supplementary information. In the course of the description given below it may be helpful to refer to the questionnaire in Appendix A.

1. <u>Measures of effectiveness</u>. Raw data representing measures of the effectiveness of secondary information services to users are obtained largely from questions in Part Three of the questionnaire. These are:

Part Three, Question 6: The distribution of points among the four given sources of secondary information should give an indication of the relative value of secondary information services as compared with other sources. While these other sources are not comprehensive, they do cover the main alternatives. To that extent the answers to this question should provide a basis by which to evaluate the effectiveness of formal secondary information services relative to other sources of secondary information. All other measures of value relate to the effectiveness of services appearing within the category "formal secondary information services."

Part Three, Question 9(a): The respondent here identifies the characteristics that in his opinion every secondary information service should possess and also indicates the degree to which the possession of these characteristics is important. When this information is combined with the degree to which the respondent is satisfied with regard to the possession of these characteristics by particular services, it becomes possible to calculate a measure of effectiveness for the given services. Information needs in questions 9 and 10 have been subdivided into current awareness, information retrieval, and other.

Part Three, Question 10: The degrees of satisfaction given for each characteristic in respect to each of the services of which the respondent makes most use provide a means for evaluating each service according to the extent to which that service achieves the standards desired of it by the respondent. This measure is obtained by combining information derived from Question 9(a) and Question 10. Two measures of value are produced for each of the most-used services.

Part Three, Question 11(a): This question is designed to produce a measure of value that will reflect the value of secondary information services both to the firm and to the individual respondent. This is done by asking the respondent to compare the ideal secondary information situation with his present situation.

Part Three, Question 11(b): The function of the answers to this question is to allow the global measures of effectiveness, which apply to all secondary information services used, to be broken down to obtain a value for each individual service.

Part Three, Question 12: The purpose of this question is to produce a measure of the value of the various secondary information services to the individual user. This is not designed to include any element of value to the firm, and it will be combined with the answers to questions 13(a) and 13(b) to obtain alternative total measures of value.

Part Three, Questions 13(a) and 13(b): Given the assumption that any decrease in time devoted to R & D work by the individuals will be a cost to the establishment, the answers to these questions allow an estimate of the value of secondary information services to the establishment to be made.

The answers to question 12, 13(a), and 13(b) form the basis of five alternative measures of effectiveness. The answers to question 12 have been labeled "Measure A," while the answers to 13(a) and 13(b) are identified as "Measure B" and "Measure D." The combination of the answers to questions 12 and 13(a) receives the appellation

"Measure C" and the corresponding measure obtained by combining the answers to question 12 and 13(b) is known as "Measure E."

Part One, Questions 9(a) and 9(b): Two further methods of assessing the value of secondary information services to the establishment consist of obtaining estimates of (i) the putative cost of obtaining the secondary information used from alternative sources, and (ii) the consumer surplus enjoyed by the establishment from the various secondary information services as measured by the maximum price the establishment would be prepared to pay for the service compared with the present price.

Part Two, Questions 4(a) and 4(b): These questions duplicate Questions 9(a) and 9(b) in Part One.

Part Three, Question 14: The aim of this question is to provide a further alternative global measure of value in terms of degree of dependency of the respondent on the secondary information services the respondent uses. This measure is defined as the "Dependence Index of Value."

Part One, Questions 4(a), 4(b), and 4(c): It would be helpful to obtain an assessment of the value of secondary information services that are used in the production of an establishment's own technical information service. By combining the answers to the three parts of this question it becomes possible to assign values to the secondary information services that are used as inputs to the internally produced secondary information service.

Part Three, Questions 1(b), 5(a), 5(b) and 15(b): In an attempt to minimize the heterogeneity of different respondents' assessments of effectiveness, the latter are weighted by data obtained from these questions.

Part One, Question 1: The first part of this question elicits information needed for the calculation of the value of a particular secondary information service to the establishment as a whole. This information is necessary to adjust the sample of individuals' response in each establishment to reflect the total number of R & D staff in the establishment.

2. Information required for the analysis of the effectiveness measures.

Part One, Question 1: The number of research and development staff and the number of information/library staff permit us to discover whether there is any correlation between degree of effectiveness and size of the establishment or size of the information/library department.

Part Two, Question 1(a) and 1(c): The answers to these questions will serve a similar function to Question 1 of Part One in that the size of the actual, or the size of the desired, budget when compared with corresponding secondary information value measures helps indicate whether size and effectiveness are related.

Part Three, Questions 1(b), 5(a) and 5(b): Information about the proportion of time spent on research and development, and on information seeking, will allow testing of the hypothesis that effectiveness is related to these variables.

Part Three, Question 1(c): The classification of effectiveness measures by the subject field of the respondent is one of the objectives of the study, and it is the purpose of this question to provide the means of classification.

Part Three, Question 2: The information elicited by this question will allow investigation of the possibility that a relationship exists between the measure of effectiveness given by a respondent and the length of time he has been employed in research and development.

Part Three, Questions 3(a) and 3(b): The answers given in questions 9 and 10 of Part Three can be weighted by the answers obtained from question 3(b) and thus permit assessment of effectiveness value based on the degree of satisfaction with the characteristics of secondary information services.

Part Three, Question 7: This question is used as an input to Question 10. The services specified are the ones about which question 10 is asked.

Part Three, Question 13(c): If the answers to questions 13(a) and 13(b) are given in percentage terms, information about the length of the work week allows the conversion of these answers, in conjunction with the answer to Question 1(b), into hours. In addition the length of the work week can be related to the respondents' effectiveness measures in order to test whether there is any apparent relationship between the two.

Part Three, Question 15(a) and 15(b): The function of this question is to provide a means of assessing whether any relationship exists between the measures of effectiveness and salary.

Part One, Questions 2 and 10 and Part Two, Question 5: By obtaining data about the number and cost of information services, two further means are provided by which the effectiveness measures in respect to each firm may be compared with the amount of secondary information taken in by a firm.

3. Descriptive information.

Part One, Questions 5 and 6: The two main items in a firm's technical information budget are staff and information services. Question 5 is an attempt to ascertain whether staff and external secondary information services are net substitutes or complements. In addition, the answers to question 5 can be compared with those of question 1(c) in Part Two to contrast the opinion of the budget allocator and the information officer. Question 6 gives an indication of the extent to which substitute services are available.

Part One, Question 7 and Part Two, Question 2: The answers to these identical questions are designed to give an indication of the "income elasticity" of different types of secondary information services. We might expect that the less effective services would be highly income-elastic.

Part One, Question 8 and Part Two, Question 3: Here again indicators of the price elasticity of different types of service are obtained.

Part One, Questions 11(a) and 11(b): These questions complement questions 8 of Part One and 3 of Part Two in that indicators are sought of the price elasticity of substitute services that are not at present obtained by the establishment.

Part Three, Questions 4(a), 4(b) and 4(c): These questions serve a similar purpose to question 1 of Part One.

Part Three, Question 9(b): One would expect those characteristics of the most-used services that the respondent has indicated in question 9(a) to be important and that in question 10 are indicated as being less than satisfactory to be the ones the respondent would desire to have improved. This question allows a test of this hypothesis.

In order to minimize bias and inconsistency in response, the decision was made to use a structured questionnaire and interview backed up by a detailed manual to be used in the training of interviewers. Use of a structured questionnaire implies that deviation from the printed questionnaire will not take place, and in conjunction with the manual this should ensure that the approach used in each interview is as nearly identical as possible. There is of course the human factor, but by impressing on each interviewer the need to ensure a standardized approach it may be possible to minimize errors.

POSSIBLE AMENDMENTS

A number of amendments to future questionnaires are suggested as follows:

Part Three, Question 11(a): There is some concern lest there might be an upward bias in the answers to this question. The question is designed to elicit a value of the effectiveness of external secondary information services that are used by the respondent on the assumption that these services are provided by the firm. The present wording of the question may stimulate the respondent's sense of loyalty to the firm and cause him to exaggerate "the value of secondary information undertaken on his behalf within the firm." A rewording of the question is recommended and might simply take the form: 11(a) Please indicate the value to you of all the secondary information services that you use on a scale from 0-50. 50 represents the value of the ideal situation in which all the information you require, but no more, is available to you exactly as you require it.

Part One, Question 4(b): The wording of this question could be improved. Without supplementary explanation by the interviewer, confusion could arise over the distinction between external and internal inputs. A more specific wording is recommended as follows: 4(b) In order to indicate the relative value of any external secondary information services that are used in the production of the internal service as compared with all other inputs, please distribute 100 points between the two.

    (i) External Secondary Information Services as an input. . . .
    (ii) All other inputs. . . .

Part One, Question 9(a): Difficulty was experienced by a number of respondents in answering this question. This appeared to arise because the number of staff, which usually formed the major part of any extra cost involved, might be the same whether the objective was to provide all secondary information used from only one abstracting service or from all services named in the question. In other words, indivisibilities were involved, and although estimates might be given of the proportion of the work time required of a qualified information officer/librarian to produce the same amount of secondary information from alternative sources, respondents were reluctant to do this for each service. This seemed to stem from the fact that some services acted as substitutes to or complements for other services and the respondent preferred to treat the named services as a group. The following wording is suggested: 9(a) If the following external sources of secondary information were no longer available to you, what would the total cost to the establishment be if the establishment were to undertake to provide all the secondary information used in these services? £. . . .

WEIGHTING

    1. <u>Background to Sample Selection</u>. Within each firm in the study a sample of R & D workers was selected to answer the interview questionnaire. For a more complete evaluation of effectiveness it was necessary to include in the sample those whose R & D activities are only a part of their total activity in the firm. The sample was drawn from those who were engaged in any way in R & D work in accordance with the definitions in the Frascatti manual.[3]

    2. <u>Definition of the Problem</u>. The problem is to convert a heterogeneous sample of respondents into a homogeneous one so as to permit meaningful aggregation. The two main aspects of heterogeneity come from variation in participation in research and development and variations in ability.

3. <u>Main Assumptions</u>. (a) Time spent on R & D work indicates value of the consequent R & D output to the firm. This leads us to conclude that where two equally paid individuals rate their dependence on an information service identically then the worker who spends more time on research and development must be assumed to have obtained the greater total benefit.

(b) Salary rates reflect differences in contributions to research and development and other areas of output. We assume that, other things being equal, the highest paid individuals contribute most to the effectiveness of an information service.

4. <u>Methods Adopted</u>. We combine the two main assumptions above to produce the following method. Our assumptions allow us to use the proportion of the individual's salary attributable to research and development as an appropriate weight. Used with the numerical indicators of effectiveness, this weight allows an assessment of the contribution to the total effectiveness of an information service in a firm's R & D work from each respondent's reply.

AGGREGATION AND CLASSIFICATION OF SECONDARY INFORMATION SERVICES

In Part One of the questionnaire, which was addressed to the information officer or librarian, details were requested of the secondary information services received by the organization. Similarly, the individual research worker was asked in Part Three to list those secondary information services he made use of. As a result a large number of titles were given.

For the purposes of the study it was necessary to divide these into a number of classes. Initially it was intended that these should be abstracts journals, titles listings, SDI (selective dissemination of information), and enquiry answering. However, it was found that the abstracts class bulked so large that it was convenient to divide it: (a) pure abstracts, that is, abstracts journals containing abstracts only, without any primary information content, and (b) abstracts in primary journals, that is, journals containing both primary information and a significant number of abstracts. (Since most primary journals contain some abstracts of condensations of material that has appeared elsewhere, it was decided to include only those in which the number of abstracts and the regularity of their inclusion was likely to encourage research workers to use them as a source of secondary information.)

Thus the basic classification of the secondary services was:

1. Titles
2. Pure abstracts
3. Abstracts in primary journals
4. SDI
5. Enquiry answering
6. Other

STRATIFICATION

In considering the stratification within these main categories, a number of aspects were considered:

1. <u>Content</u>. That is, the type of material referred to or listed by the service, for example, patents, reports, periodical articles, etc. This was considered an important aspect since it might reflect differing usages and requirements. It was therefore selected for stratification and these categories were formed: 0—Reports; 1—Patents; 2—Standards and specifications; 3—Conferences; 4—General (i.e., including all the above categories) and other. Thus items would be included only in categories 0, 1, 2, and 3 if they were solely devoted to reports, patents, standards and specifications, or conferences respectively.

2. <u>Nationality</u>. Since much of the study of the cost-effectiveness of information services will be by national bodies and therefore on a national basis, a nationality category was considered essential. For the purpose of the study the following were chosen: 0—United Kingdom; 1—North America; 2—Remainder of Europe; 3—Other. It was unnecessary to subdivide the remainder of Europe into individual nations because of the small number of services emanating from there that were listed.

3. <u>Arrangement</u>. That is, whether the entries provided by the service are arranged by subject, author, by first word of title, etc. Although this would be of interest it was not considered an important distinction, particularly as the subject arrangement may vary from highly specific terms with few items listed under them to broad categories with a large number of items listed under each. In addition, there is little uniformity, with individual information services often using more than one mode of arrangement. Since, therefore, it did not seem possible to establish unambiguous and useful categories, no stratification by arrangement was attempted.

4. <u>Language</u>. This was of minor consequence since only a few of the services listed are published in other than the English language. However, the language of the documents referred to by the secondary services normally varied widely. Only in very few, clearly defined instances did the coverage not include a wide range of foreign-language material, preventing clear classification.

5. <u>Subject field</u>. Initially this was considered at least as important as content and nationality since it could be used both in relation to the discipline of the individual research workers and for the comparison between services. Subject categories were chosen, after considerable experiments, but it was found impracticable to apply them owing to the number required if they were to be useful and the large number of marginal cases.

6. <u>Inclusion of subject indexes</u>. While this was accepted as an important aspect, it was not used for stratification for two reasons. In the first place, subject indexes and arrangement by subject are in some instances alternatives, and arrangement by subject had not been chosen for the reason given in point 3. Second and more importantly, there is often great difficulty in deciding whether a subject index is included or not. If the index is not included with each issue of the abstracts journal (these being the publications for which the inclusion of an index is most important), but instead an annual index is provided at a much later date, it is difficult to decide whether the index is included in any real sense or not.

7. <u>Indicative or informative</u> (that is, merely indicating in the abstract the content of the document or reproducing the most important information provided by the document). This is again an interesting aspect that, in practice, could not be included. It would have required a detailed study of all the services listed to establish which type of abstract they provided. Even with detailed study, however, this was unlikely to be satisfactory since many services provide a mixture of informative and indicative abstracts.

It is possible, of course, to discover many other characteristics of secondary information services. The inclusion or noninclusion of back references had to be excluded on practical grounds as in point 7.

COSTING MEASUREMENTS

Cost-effectiveness requires that the costs to be taken into account be defined and then related to the effectiveness measures adopted. Many practical and conceptual problems arise in this context and this section sets out the reasoning behind the practical procedures in the Cost Manual (Appendix C).

Costs

The definition of costs used here is the amount of resources in money terms that is utilized in the production of a specified output, given that some alternative use may be found for the resources if they were not so employed. The problem is to allocate scarce resources to the most profitable uses and it can be assumed that there is always a cost in terms of opportunities associated with a particular course of action.

In principle the method of approach is to isolate the resources that are devoted to the production of secondary information and place a monetary value on them. However, in practice the exact determination of these resources raises certain problems, the best-known example being the case where the same set of resources is used in the production of different services; in the information context this is usually the performance of several tasks by a particular individual or group of individuals. Another similar type of problem arises where the information system is situated in or is closely connected with a library and in some ways is indistinguishable from it. In such circumstances the principle adopted is that the appropriate cost to be calculated is a form of long-run marginal cost, which may be defined as those costs that would ultimately cease to exist were the particular output under consideration to be discounted. This is almost equivalent to the determination of those costs that can be attributed in some rational or a priori manner to the outputs under consideration. This form of approach will involve the allocation of joint costs in most cases.

The determination of costs is of such complexity and has so many interpretations placed on it that it is necessary for a certain amount of discretion to be exercised from time to time. It is as important to isolate and standardize this discretionary element as far as possible by setting down general principles as it is to establish theoretical principles that serve as the ideals with respect to the quality and usefulness of the data collected. The practical instances where discretion is necessary are discussed in Appendix C and only the principles for the use of discretion are dealt with here.

The costs that are applicable for the purposes of cost-effectiveness can be isolated at three levels: the total cost of the information system, this cost broken down by type of output where more than one service is produced, and costs separated by activities within the production of each service. The first of these will give the basis upon which to evaluate the cost-effectiveness of the information system as a whole, the second will provide the cost-effectiveness by service and permit aggregation across systems by service, and the third will provide information upon which to base estimates of marginal cost; this is explained more fully in the following section.

In the cases where the information system is part of a larger organization and produces several outputs then a multistage estimation procedure will be necessary: (a) isolate the costs relevant to the information system as a whole; (b) isolate the cost of each service produced; and (c) breakdown the cost of producing each service according to various predetermined classifications of activity.

A full description of the problems likely to be encountered and the principles to be applied is contained in Appendix C. It need only be stressed here that the costs which are identified and estimated using the methods as set out are purely intended for the purposes of assessing cost-effectiveness. As such they may not appeal to accountants and cost accountants, who have different objectives in mind when assembling cost data, nor even perhaps to economic purists who may regard some of the methods as rather ad hoc; however, the methods are based on the experience of over twenty cost studies and constitute the best compromise which the team could devise. The fact is that we must lay aside many of our purist ideals when coming to grips with reality in the attempt to provide at lease partial answers to complex and sometimes insoluble questions.

NOTES

1. American Economic Review, Papers and Proceedings, 1965, pp. 481-94.
2. Raymond M. Hughes, "Report to the Association of American Colleges," January 1925.
3. Measurement of Scientific and Technical Activities: Proposed Standard Practice for Surveys of Research and Experimental Development [the Frascatti Manual] (Paris: O.E.C.D., 1970) pp. 147-48.

APPENDIX TO CHAPTER 3: THE SAMPLE

The sampling procedure involved a random sampling of firms that conduct research and development. The sample was divided into those firms in the Aslib Directory that were the largest information users, in terms of stocks of current periodicals, and others.

The resulting number of firms visited was 93, split between the different industries as shown in Table 3.1.

The sample was further stratified when individual R & D workers were selected for interview from these firms. Table 3.2 shows the total number of respondents in each industry. This latter selection was conducted randomly wherever possible. Of the individual respondents, 71.4 percent were thus randomly selected (see Table 3.3).

The various effectiveness measures were examined to see whether the individuals who were not selected randomly introduced any systematic bias into the results. Table 3.4 shows that there is

TABLE 3.1

The Distribution of the Sample by Industry

Industry	Amount of Information Used	Number of Firms
Agriculture	Small	15
	Large	4
Aircraft	Small	12
	Large	3
Chemicals	Small	16
	Large	4
Electrical engineering	Small	14
	Large	3
Textiles	Small	17
	Large	5
Total		93

Source: Compiled by the authors.

no systematic upward or downward bias in the results caused by the difference in selection procedures. In the light of this it is concluded that the selection provides a reasonably satisfactory basis.

The distribution of respondents across a wide range of different subject fields and disciplines is shown in Table 3.5. This demonstrates

TABLE 3.2

Total Individual Respondents by Industry

Industry	Number
Agriculture	64
Aircraft	54
Chemicals	57
Electrical engineering	82
Textiles	60

Source: Compiled by the author.

TABLE 3.3

Individual Respondents by Method of Selection

Selection	Number	Percent of Total
Randomly selected	225	71.4
Nonrandomly selected	87	27.6
Not known how selected	3	1.0
Total	315	100.0

Source: Compiled by the authors.

that the largest groups of R & D worker samples fall under the general heading of chemistry, followed closely by electrical and mechanical engineering. In the following text and tables the classifications used are the broader "discipline" groups. Under these headings interesting results emerge concerning, for example, the average salary of chemists

TABLE 3.4

Value of A, B, and D Values and X-Factor Secondary Information by Method of Selection

Randomness	B	D	A	X-Factor Secondary Information
Random	223	177	335	30.2
Nonrandom	151	167	427	33.9

Source: Compiled by the authors.

By Randomness—Unweighted 0-50 Value and 0-50 Dependence		
Randomness	Unweighted 0-50 Value	Unweighted 0-50 Dependence
Random	28.1	19.5
Nonrandom	26.3	20.4

Source: Compiled by the authors.

TABLE 3.5

Sample of Individual Respondents by Field of Interest

	Number of Individuals	Total Number of Individuals	Percent of Respondents
General chemistry	27		
Inorganic chemistry	2		
Organic chemistry	16		
Dyestuff chemistry	4		
Paint/resins/surface coatings	1		
Analytic chemistry	2		
Electrochemistry	4		
Chemical engineering	7		
Biochemistry	5		
Physical chemistry	5	73	23.9
Microbiology	2		
Biology	4		
Medicine	2	8	2.6
Pharmacology	2		
Pharmaceutical production	1		
Pharmaceutical technology	1	4	1.3
Agricultural chemistry	22		
Agricultural botany	2	24	7.8
Food and drugs chemistry	10	10	3.3
Textile production	4		
Textile technology	10		
Textile display	1		
Textile fibers	6		
Textile chemistry	8	29	9.5
Metal finishing	6		
Metallurgy	9	15	4.9
Silicon	1	1	0.3
Physics	5		
Accoustics	1		
Friction	1		
Thermal physics	2		
Optics	3		
Lubricants	2	14	4.6
Fuel technology	4	4	1.3

	Number of Individuals	Total Number of Individuals	Percent of Respondents
General mechanical engineering	33		
Mechanical engineering components	3		
Mechanical engineering design	1		
Hydraulics	3		
Marine engineering	1		
Mechanical engineering production	3	44	14.4
General electrical engineering	12		
Electromagnetics	2		
General electronics	22		
Communications	3		
Electromechanics	8		
Electrical engineering design	2	49	16.0
Computer technology	2		
Computer hardware	5		
Control technology	1	8	2.6
Instrumentation	3		
Electrical instrumentation	2	5	1.7
Aerodynamics	2		
Aero engineering	1		
Aero components	2		
Aero engines	1	6	2.0
Quality control	2	2	0.7
Economics	2	2	0.7
Systems analysis	2		
Mathematics	1	3	1.0
Other	5	5	1.7
Totals		306	100.3

Source: Compiled by the authors.

and the average percentage of total time spent on research and development by mechanical engineers. While such findings are of interest, it must be emphasized that the individuals were not randomly sampled upon a basis of disciplines and the results emerging from the analysis should be treated with more caution than those for which the study is more soundly based, that is, for results by industry.

Bearing such qualifications in mind, it is possible to examine certain findings from the survey concerning the salary, age, and distribution of working time of the R & D workers.

The results concerning salaries should perhaps be given special note, since the salary of an individual is one of the chief constituents of the weight given to his effectiveness measures. Figure 3.1 shows that the majority of R & D workers earn between £1,200 and £3,000. The mean salary of the respondents across industries was found to be £2,261.

A more detailed breakdown is shown in Table 3.6, where the average salaries are classified by industries. The relatively low average salary in electrical engineering should be noted.

The distribution of average salaries over disciplines (Table 3.7) shows several interesting features, notably the high average salary among pharmacologists, aeronautics and medical workers, and the relatively low average salaries in physics.

As is illustrated by Figure 3.2, the bulk of the R & D workers are between the ages of 25 and 50 with a sharp decline after the age of 50. The average age over all industries was found to be 37. A breakdown by industries (see Table 3.8) reveals no marked deviations from this mean, although attention may be drawn to the low average age in the electrical engineering industry and the high average age in the chemical industry. A higher average age is encountered in "small" firms in all industries, but the difference is slight, on average two years. Predictably, there is a high correlation between age and salary (Figure 3.3). In view of this high correlation, however, it would be expected that the weights (dependent upon salary) that are given to the effectiveness measures of old men would be greater than those of the younger R & D workers. This factor should be given consideration in examination of the effectiveness results.

In addition to their date of birth, respondents were asked the number of years they had worked in research and development (Tables 3.8 and 3.9). There are no startling variations between industries, although it could perhaps be mentioned that the average number of years in research and development in electrical engineering is lower than that in other industries. The findings are similar for large and small firms, despite the slight divergence in the average age. In the case of disciplines, more exceptional results emerge, notably the high average number of R & D years in aeronautics, followed by

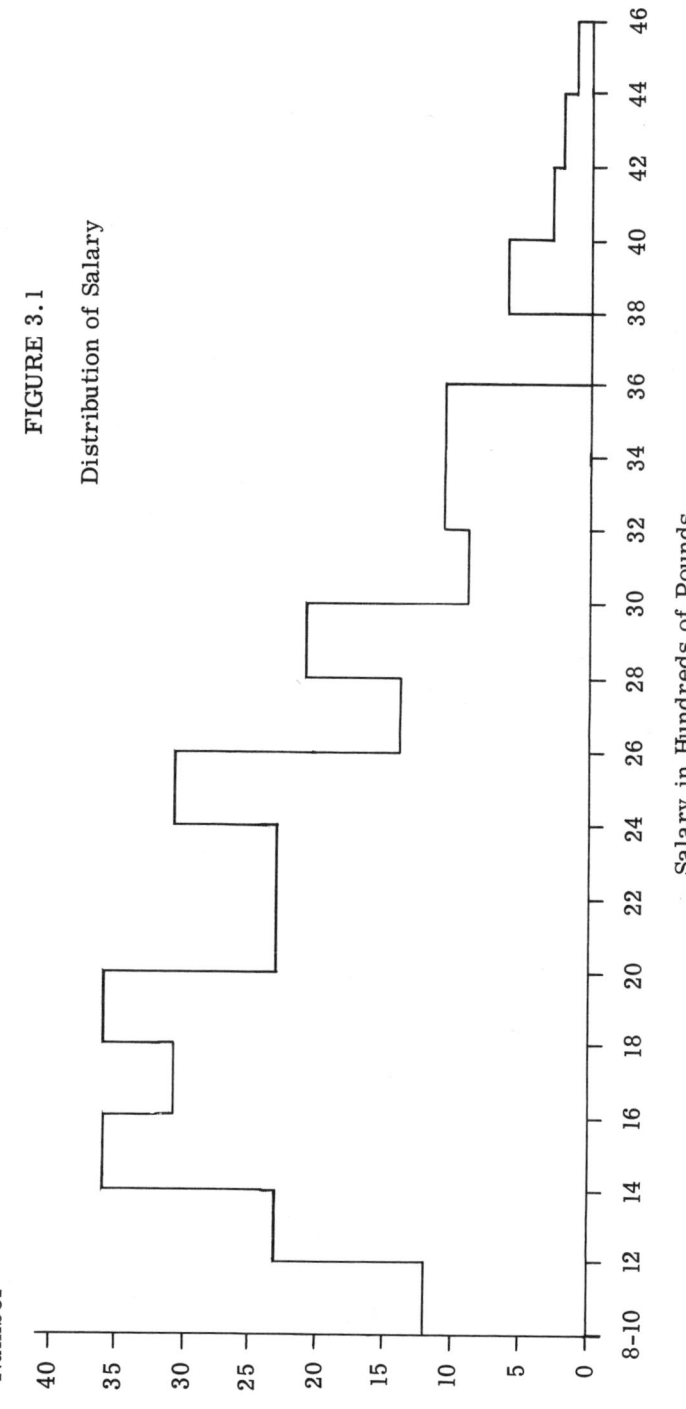

FIGURE 3.1

Distribution of Salary

Salary in Hundreds of Pounds

Note: In addition there were 2 at £5,000; 2 at £6,000; 1 at £10,200; and 1 at £14,000.

Source: Compiled by the authors.

TABLE 3.6

Average Salaries of R & D Workers by Industry

Industry	Average Salary in Pounds
Small Information	
Agriculture	£2,064
Aircraft	2,169
Chemicals	2,352
Electrical engineering	1,955
Textiles	2,869[a]
	2,235[a]
Large Information	
Agriculture	2,497
Aircraft	2,345
Chemicals	3,014
Electrical engineering	1,838
Textiles	2,512
Total	
Agriculture	2,267
Aircraft	2,205
Chemicals	2,602
Electrical engineering	1,922
Textiles	2,710[a]
	2,363[b]
Overall average	£2,261

Note: Respondents to this question = 95.9 percent.

[a]Including two extreme values.
[b]Excluding the extreme values.

Source: Compiled by the authors.

instruments (measurement) and pharmacology, and the relatively low average number of years found in the physics and computers/control disciplines.

A number of facts emerge concerning the distribution of the working time of R & D workers. Figure 3.4 shows that the majority of respondents spend a large proportion of their time on research and development (about 70 percent on average) and that a great number

TABLE 3.7

Average Salary per Discipline Group

Discipline	Average Salary (in pounds)
Chemistry	2,259
Medical/biological	2,725
Pharmacology/pharmaceutics	3,675
Agriculture	2,186
Food and drink	2,480
Textiles	2,494a
Material—metal/metallurgy/ metal finishing	1,856
Material—nonmetal and nontextile	2,000b
Physics/accoustics	1,978c
Fuel	2,167b
Mechanical engineering	2,202
Electrical engineering/communications	2,081
Computers/control	1,810
Instruments/measurement	2,538
Aeronautics	2,933
Production	1,925b
Management	2,550b
Mathematics/statistics	2,133b
Other	2,200

[a]Excludes salary of £14,000 (new average £2,891).
[b]Less than five observations.
[c]Excludes salary of £10,120 (new average £2,560).

Source: Compiled by the authors.

spend between 90 and 100 percent of their time on research and development. A more detailed classification (Table 3.10) reveals that workers in "large" information firms, without exception, spend a greater percentage of their total time on research and development. It should be noted, however, that in "small" electrical engineering firms, the percentage of time spent on research and development is almost as great as in "large" electrical engineering. The greatest percentage of working time spent on research and development is found in the chemical industry.

FIGURE 3.2

Distribution amongst Respondents of Age

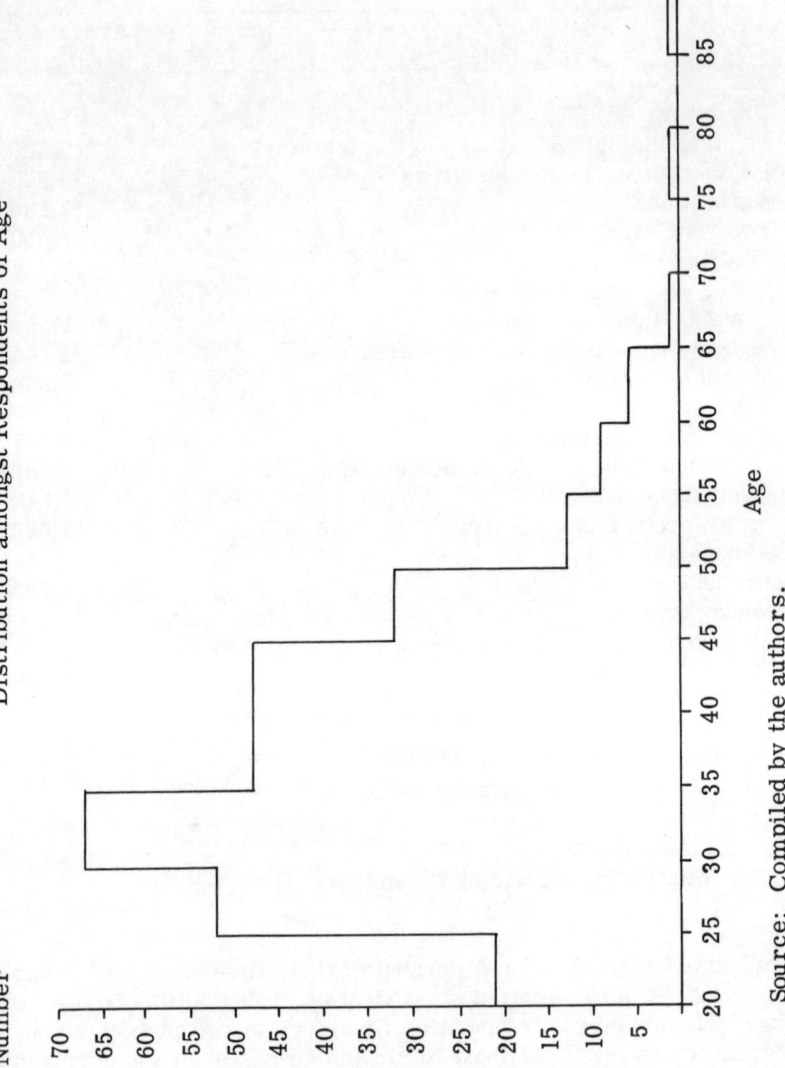

Source: Compiled by the authors.

FIGURE 3.3

Salary and Age of Respondents

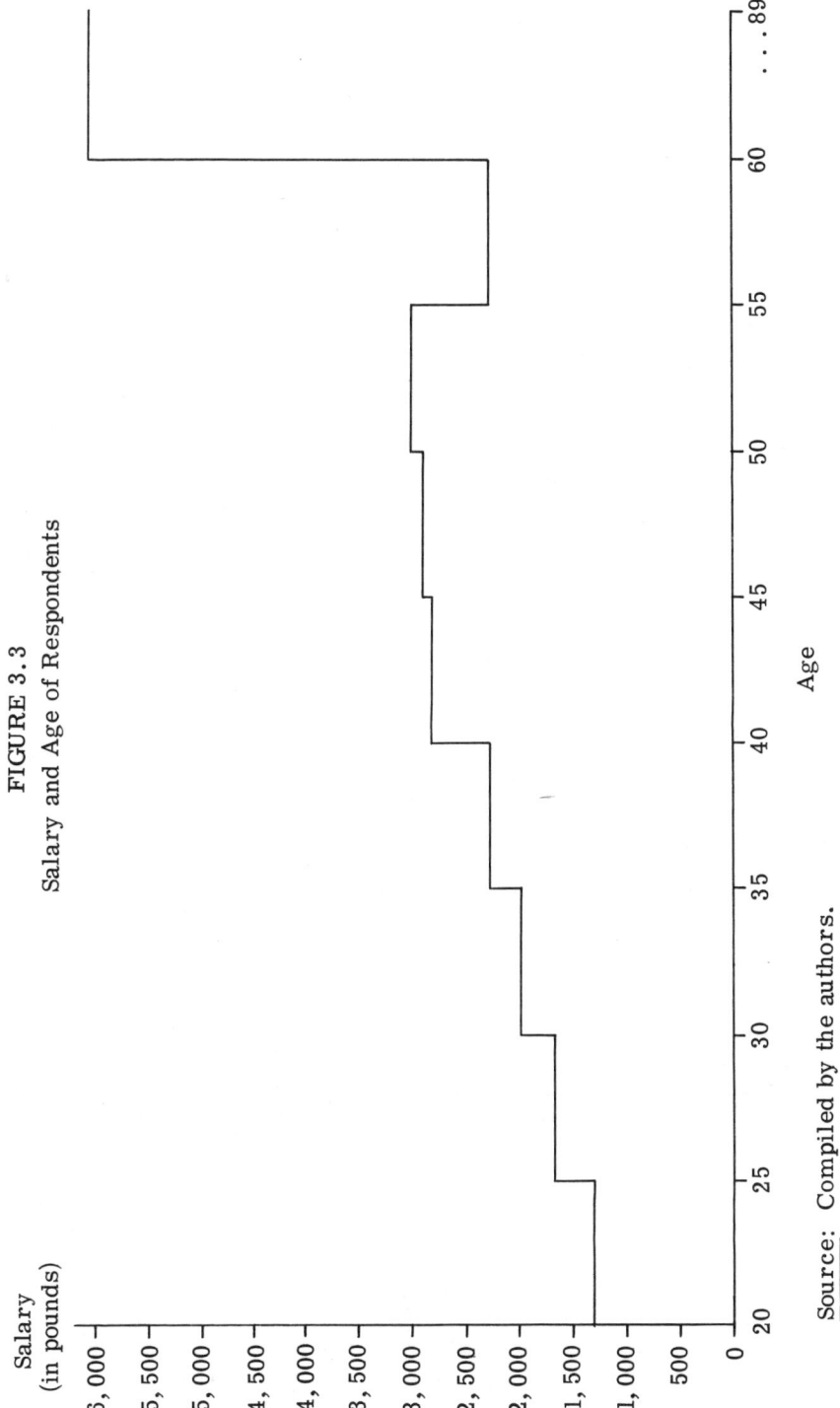

Source: Compiled by the authors.

TABLE 3.8

Average Number of Years in Research and Development
and Mean Age of Each Respondent, by Industry and
Large/Small Firm

Industry	Amount of Information Used	Average Number of Years in R & D		Mean Age	
Agriculture	Large		12		36
		12		37	
	Small		12		37
Aircraft	Large		15		38
		13		38	
	Small		12		38
Chemicals	Large		11		39
		13		40	
	Small		15		40
Electrical engineering	Large		9		32
		10		34	
	Small		11		35
Textiles	Large		14		37
		13		39	
	Small		13		39
All industries	Large		12		36
	Small		12		38

Source: Compiled by the authors.

The only remarkable average proportion of time spent in research and development is found in the food and drink industry (see Table 3.11). It can be concluded that, with a few exceptions, the result found concerning all respondents—that the majority of workers spend a large proportion of their time on research and development—is broadly true in all industries and disciplines.

The relationship between the proportion of time spent on research and development and the percentage of that R & D time spent on information seeking is portrayed in Figure 3.5. Here it is interesting to note that R & D workers spending 50-100 percent of their time on research and development spend no more of their R & D time on information than those engaged in research and development for only 0-50 percent of their time. If the relationship were expressed in

TABLE 3.9

Number of Years in Research and Development,
by Discipline

Discipline	Average Number of Years in R & D
Chemistry	12
Medical/biological	11
Pharmacology	16
Agriculture	13
Food	11
Textiles	13
Metal materials/metallurgy	13
Nonmetal materials	35*
Physics/acoustics	9
Fuel	8*
Mechanical engineering	11
Electrical engineering	11
Computers/control	8
Instruments/measurement	19
Aeronautics	28
Production	31*
Management	12*
Mathematics/statistics	11*
Other	14

*Less than five observations.

Source: Compiled by the authors.

hours, however, those spending 50-100 percent of their time on research and development would obviously be spending more hours on information work than the other. Figure 3.5 suggests, however, that whether a R & D worker spends 1 percent or 100 percent of his time on research and development, he will spend only between 10 percent and 35 percent of that on information work.

A further result is given by the relationship between R & D time spent on information work and information time spent on secondary information (Figure 3.6). R & D workers spending a greater percentage of their time on information do not spend a significantly greater

FIGURE 3.4

Distribution amongst Respondents of Time Spent on Research and Development

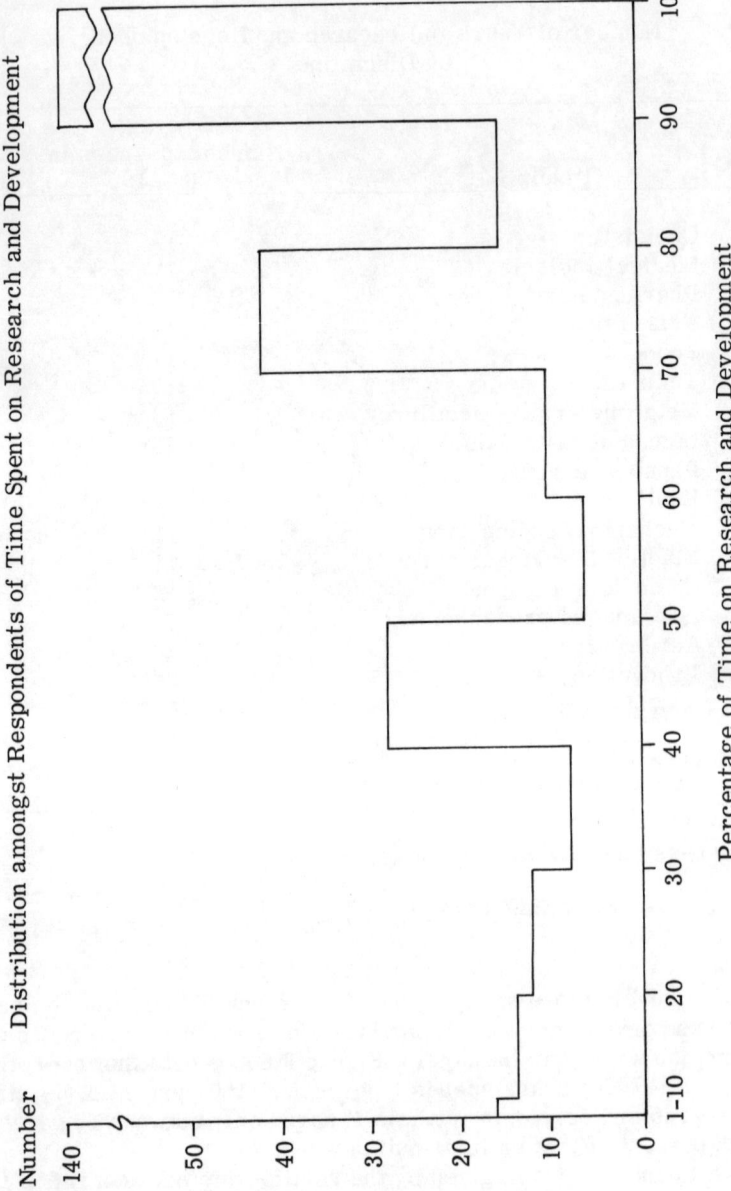

Percentage of Time on Research and Development

Source: Compiled by the authors.

TABLE 3.10

Average Percentage of Total Time Spent on Research and Development, by Industry

Industry	Amount of Information Used	Percentage of Time Spent
Agriculture	Large	89
	Small	64
	Total	75
Aircraft	Large	91
	Small	70
	Total	74
Chemicals	Large	94
	Small	75
	Total	82
Electrical engineering	Large	80
	Small	76
	Total	77
Textiles	Large	84
	Small	60
	Total	70

Source: Compiled by the authors.

TABLE 3.11

Percentage Time Spent on Research and Development, by Discipline

Discipline	Percentage Time Spent on R & D
Chemistry	79.6
Medical/biological	86.3
Pharmacology/pharmaceutics	93.8*
Agriculture	78.7
Food and drink	48.0
Textile	63.9
Material—metal/metallurgy/metal finishing	63.3
Material—Nonmetal and Nontextile	100.0*
Physics/acoustics	76.4
Fuel	93.3*
Mechanical engineering	84.1
Electrical engineering/communications	70.3
Computers/control	80.6
Instruments/measurement	84.0
Aeronautics	66.7
Production	15.0*
Management	18.0*
Mathematics/statistics	100.0*
Other	80.4

*Less than five observations.

Source: Compiled by the authors.

FIGURE 3.5

Time Spent on Information Work
related to Time Spent on
Research and Development

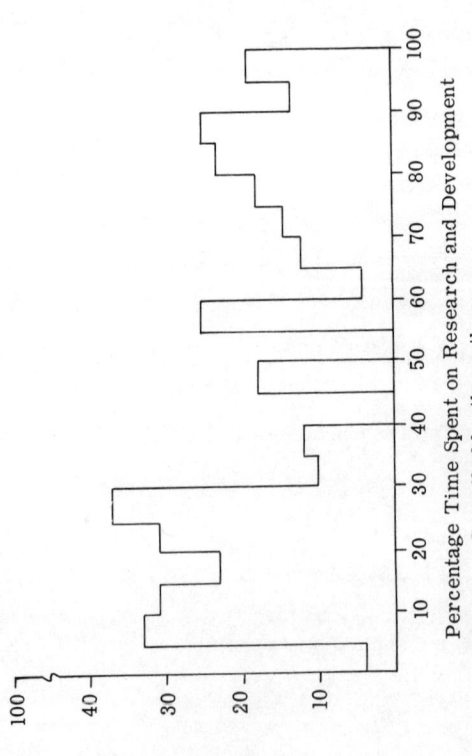

Source: Compiled by the authors.

FIGURE 3.6

Relationship between R & D Time Spent on Information
and Information Time Spent on Secondary Information

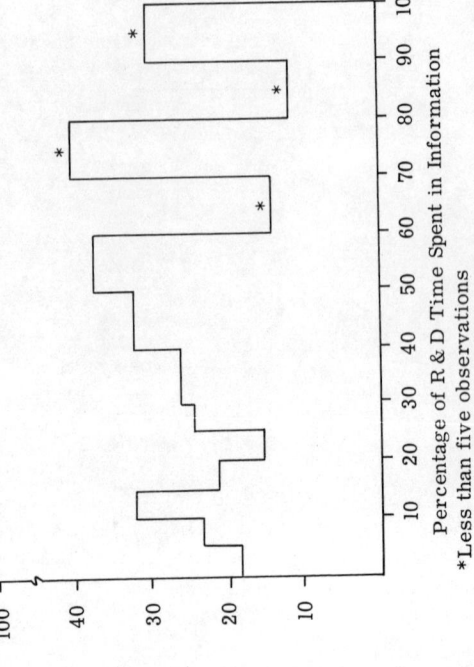

*Less than five observations
Source: Compiled by the authors.

TABLE 3.12

Information Expenditure and R & D Effort

Industry	Average Number of R & D Workers per Firm	Average Information Expenditure per Firm (£)	Average Number of Professional Information Staff per Firm	Average Information Expenditure per R & D Worker per Firm (£)	Average of Professional Information Staff per R & D Worker
Agriculture					
Large information	179	11,464	13.5	96	.08
Small information	13	4,081	3.1	192	.23
All firms	47	8,452	5.2	114	.12
Aircraft					
Large information	1,125	4,500	8.5	18	.01
Small information	163	4,359	2.8	42	.02
All firms	264	4,406	3.5	38	.01
Chemical					
Large information	269	59,000	16.0	275	.06
Small information	12	3,348	1.4	279	.14
All firms	63	12,623	3.8	276	.07
Electrical Engineering					
Large information	176	42,000	9.3	256	.05
Small	74	2,177	1.1	86	.02
All firms	91	8,304	2.5	177	.03
Textiles					
Large information	146	23,860	17.2	164	.12
Small information	5	1,011	0.3	171	.06
All firms	36	7,024	4.0	165	.11
All Industries					
Large information	294	30,239	14.9	170	.05
Small information	54	2,921	1.7	86	.03
All firms	98	8,312	3.8	133	.04

Source: Compiled by the authors.

percentage of their time on secondary information. Between 19 and 37 percent of information time is spent solely on secondary information. The relationships suggested by Figures 3.5 and 3.6 are broadly proportionate, that is, time spent on information is proportional to time spent on research and development, and time spent on secondary information is proportional to time spent on all information.

Lastly, Table 3.12 offers detailed results on information expenditure and the numbers of R & D workers in different industries. By definition, "large" firms would be expected to have bigger information expenditures. This is borne out by the results in all industries except, perhaps surprisingly, the aircraft industry, where "large" and "small" firms have almost the same information expenditure per firm. A second finding is that without exception "large" firms have a significantly greater average number of R & D workers per firm than "small" firms, and here the aircraft industry far outstrips other industries. An interesting point is the relatively high correlation between information budgets and the number of professional information staff, although it should be noted that the information expenditure includes the salaries of this information staff. It is noteworthy that, although information expenditure of "large" firms is large, in four of the five industries the average information expenditure per R & D worker in "small" firms is greater than that in the "large" firms.

CHAPTER 4

RESULTS

EFFECTIVENESS RESULTS

The purpose of this chapter is to present the results of the study. In some instances measures will appear in money terms; in others they are indexes. Before proceeding to examine the different measures of effectiveness of secondary information and their various characteristics, we will examine the relative importance of the different methods of acquiring secondary information.

There are several methods by which secondary information can be presented. The most important method for this study is that of published secondary information. However, the information contained in primary journals may find its way into what may be termed trade literature, usually distributed for commercial advertising purposes giving details of new processes and equipment, but incorporating information regarding test results and allied data.

Information may be transmitted orally, both between colleagues within firms and in wider circles. Information found originally in primary journals is passed on both formally and informally through symposia and conferences. To consider the economics of published secondary information in isolation would lead to difficulties of interpretation. Questions were asked to elicit the relative importance of the different kinds of secondary information. In this way secondary information of the published kind is seen in a more general context.

The responses, weighted to account for variations in quality and quantity of R & D work done indicate in aggregate the relative importance of published secondary information, trade literature, personal contact both within and outside the establishment. Several ways of illustrating these results are useful: by information need, discipline of the respondents, and industrial classification. Respondents were asked to distribute 100 points between the four competing secondary services. These responses were then weighted by the proportion of the respondent's salary derived solely from his work on research and development and aggregates were calculated for the firms within the sample and the complete population. The comments elsewhere regarding statistical validity should, of course, remain prominent in considering the implications of these results. The aggregate marks were converted to percentages of the totals allocated by each stratified class. Those percentages are presented in Tables 4.1, 4.2, and 4.3.

Table 4.1 suggests that those with needs solely for information retrieval rely more on published secondary information than those who merely wish to be kept up to date. It confirms previous findings of information scientists that personal contact is a more generally used source of secondary information than are abstracts, titles lists, and the other forms of published secondary information.

One interesting aspect of these results is the low value given to published secondary information by those who have a general need for information. The most obvious explanation is the rise in personal contact outside the establishment. That is, those R & D workers whose information need stretches beyond finding specific pieces of information or being kept up to date may build up a large number of external contacts to supplement the conventional sources of secondary information.

Turning now to the discipline groupings, we observe in Table 4.2 the considerable intradisciplinary variations. Published secondary information has marks ranging from 22.5 percent to 44.7 percent, trade literature from 6 percent to 36.3 percent and personal contact inside and outside the firm from 19.3 percent to 33.2 percent and from 11.9 percent to 32.5 percent respectively.

It is interesting to notice that for chemists, published secondary information is as important as personal contact, a reflection perhaps of the large flow of published secondary information in this field. It is surprising, however, to observe how poorly physicists and electrical engineers rate published secondary information.

The most important of the results and the most accurate are those given for the industrial classifications. Superior accuracy is derived from the method of sampling, which was performed on an industry basis. Thus results based on an aggregation of data by industrial classification will have greater accuracy than those derived from other classifications. Table 4.3 shows the considerable variation over the industries sampled. The relative positions of agriculture and electrical engineering are at first glance suprising. It might have been imagined that with a much higher research expenditure the electrical engineering industry would have relied more heavily than the agriculture industry on the systematized presentation of published secondary information rather than on the haphazard and fortuitous arrival of trade literature. It is also interesting to note that there is very little interindustry difference in the value assigned to total personal contact.

TABLE 4.1

The Relationship between the Value of Published
Secondary Information and Other Sources of
Secondary Information Displayed with Respect
to the Type of Information Need
(percentages are of total allocation of marks, weighted)

Information Need	Published Secondary Information	Trade Literature	Personal Contact Inside Establishment	Personal Contact Outside Establishment
Information retrieval	38.9	20.1	27.4	13.7
Current Awareness	35.6	13.9	33.2	17.4
Both	33.8	21.4	24.8	20.7

Source: Compiled by the authors.

MEASURES OF EFFECTIVENESS AND DEPENDENCE

There are two basic methods of presentation for the measures of effectiveness of published secondary information that have been determined from Part Three of the questionnaire. The first is the set of average values for the individuals in the population; the second is a breakdown by industry and type of service used. Aggregate values for industries were determined by grossing up the results to take account of the sampling procedures.

Average Individual Values

The measures are seen in Tables 4.4-4.9, displayed with respect to stratifications of the users.

Measure A gives the increase in salary that the respondents would require to compensate them for a withdrawal of secondary information. This is intended to be a measure in money of the value of secondary information in terms of job satisfaction and promotion prospects.

Measures B and D derive from the questions regarding the allocation of working time between R & D work and information work. Measure B indicates the extra value of the research and development

TABLE 4.2

The Relationship between the Value of Published
Secondary Information and Other Sources of
Secondary Information Displayed with Respect to
the Discipline of the Respondents
(percentages are of total allocation of marks, weighted)

Discipline Group	Published Secondary Information	Trade Literature	Personal Contact Inside Establishment	Personal Contact Outside Establishment
Chemistry	40.2	19.6	24.9	15.3
Medical/ Biological	44.7	6.0	33.2	16.4
Agriculture— animals/ plants	37.4	18.5	19.3	24.7
Food	36.3	15.4	29.2	19.1
Textile	28.4	20.8	30.9	20.0
Material— metal/ metallurgy/ metal finishing	28.5	20.9	27.4	23.1
Physics/acoustics	22.5	21.2	23.9	32.5
Mechanical engineering	35.2	18.9	20.5	25.3
Electrical engineering/ communications	27.3	30.0	26.4	16.4
Computers/ control	27.5	36.3	24.3	11.9
All	34.3	20.6	24.9	20.2

Source: Compiled by the authors.

TABLE 4.3

The Relationship between the Value of Published
Secondary Information and Other Sources of
Secondary Information Displayed with Respect to
the Industry Classifications
(percentages are of total allocation of marks, weighted)

Industry	Published Secondary Information	Trade Literature	Personal Contact Inside Establishment	Personal Contact Outside Establishment
Agriculture	40.7	16.1	22.8	20.4
Chemicals	40.5	15.4	26.0	18.1
Aircraft	35.6	17.1	24.6	22.7
Textiles	30.4	22.7	28.6	18.4
Engineering	23.4	30.9	24.4	21.2
All	34.3	20.6	24.9	20.2

Source: Compiled by the authors.

achieved as a result of the availability of secondary information. Implicitly, Measure B assumes that the information obtained from secondary information can be obtained in other ways. Measure D relaxes this assumption. It is derived from the extra hours of R&D work that would be required if secondary information is withdrawn. The various measures C_i and E_i combine the values B, D, and A in various ways. The measures C_1, C_2, C_3, C_4 and E_1, E_2, E_3, E_4 represent combinations of A and B and A and D linearly where the coefficient of B or D varies thus: 1, 0.75, 0.5, 0.25.

Finally the individual respondents indicated, on the scale 0-50, their dependence on secondary information. From this an index of dependence is derived which is that mark weighted by the part of the respondent's salary applicable to his R&D work.

While the A, B, and D measures are comparable with each other, they are not directly comparable with the C and E measures without making certain allowances. Although Measure C is derived from the sum of A and B for each individual and Measure E from the sum of A and D for each individual, inspection of the figures shows that (A + B) and (A + D) tend to be in excess of C and E respectively. This is because the A, B, C, D, and E values are aggregate and are grossed up over different numbers of respondents.

To the extent that our interest lies solely in external secondary information services our attention should be focused on the C and E measures. If, however, we desire to consider all secondary information services, the A, B, D, and Dependence Index measures will be relevant. It may be of interest to compare the sets of values in order to obtain an indication of the value placed on internally provided secondary information services.

Effectiveness Measures and Information Need

Table 4.4 indicates the measures outlined above with respect to users whose needs for information are either purely retrieval, purely current awareness, or both. It is immediately noticeable that the values associated with retrieval alone are very much less than for current awareness. It is clear also that a major part of the values of C and D come from the value of A. No significant difference in ranking between C_1, C_2, C_3, C_4, or E_1, E_2, E_3, E_4 occurs as a result of using different coefficients in their calculation.

Those with current awareness needs only, while giving the highest overall value to the secondary information, appear least dependent upon it. This accords with the view that current awareness enhances promotion prospects and adds to the satisfaction of the work, whereas retrieval is designed for success with a particular project.

Effectiveness Measures and Type of Work

It is clear from Table 4.5 that those engaged in research and research and development together place a higher value on secondary information than those solely engaged in development. If Measure D is used, R & D users give considerably higher values than those engaged in only one of these activities. This suggests that the information required by development workers is more difficult to obtain from other sources and that when secondary information is not available the quality of the work must suffer.

Again, the Dependence Index is consistent with the B and D values. The use of different coefficients slightly alters the rankings, but these differences are not significant.

Effectiveness Measures and Age of Respondents

The respondents over 55 gave extreme replies to many questions. In aggregation the respondents' replies were conditioned by their large salaries. These respondents, having many commitments, were unable to find extra time to pursue information work and consequently the quality of their R & D work fell considerably if secondary information was withdrawn. This is reflected in the much higher E values than C

TABLE 4.4

Different Measures Displayed with Respect to Information Need
(average values per individual)

Information Need	A	B	C1	C2	C3	C4	D	E1	E2	E3	E4	Dependence	C Rank	E Rank	Dependence Rank
Information retrieval only	160	102	234	212	190	168	70	197	181	165	149	25559	3	3	2
Current awareness only	517	70	540	523	506	488	55	568	555	541	527	24492	1	1	3
Both	372	212	536	489	441	393	191	527	480	435	387	30338	2	2	1

Note: Measure A: increase in salary required to compensate for loss of secondary information. Measure B: derived from adjustment of hours devoted to R & D and information if secondary information is withdrawn. Measure C_i: $A + iB$, $i = 1, 0.75, 0.5, 0.25$. Measure D: derived from readjustment of hours after loss of secondary information to achieve same output. Measure E_i: $A + iD$, $i = 1, 0.75, 0.5, 0.25$. Dependence: derived from weighted 0-50 mark for dependence.

As not all respondents gave replies to provide A, B, and D, the C_i and E_i measures only derive from respondents where both A and B or A and D replies were received.

Source: Compiled by the author

TABLE 4.5

Different Measures Displayed with Respect to Type of Work
(average values per individual)

Type of Work	A	B	C1	C2	C3	C4	D	E1	E2	E3	E4	Dependence	C Rank	E Rank	Dependence Rank
Research	406	236	553	504	455	406	249	434	404	374	344	38967	2	2-3	1
Development	331	220	446	403	360	309	171	459	415	371	328	23435	3	2-3	3
Research and development	402	182	577	533	489	447	195	616	562	511	455	33796	1	1	2

Note: See Table 4.4 for explanation of measures A, B, C_i, D, E_i, and Dependence.

Source: Compiled by the authors.

TABLE 4.6

Different Measures Displayed with Respect to Age of Respondents
(average values per individual)

Age	A	B	C_1	C_2	C_3	C_4	D	E_1	E_2	E_3	E_4	Dependence	C Rank	E Rank	Dependence Rank
21-25	279	126	475	444	412	367	62	458	431	404	377	18099	4	5	8
26-30	256	185	343	313	283	230	133	322	293	266	238	24474	7	8	7
31-35	278	203	444	399	353	305	182	464	419	374	329	26521	6	6	5
36-40	373	159	461	429	397	365	216	415	387	359	331	24693	5	7	6
41-45	566	94	490	471	451	431	75	528	506	484	463	35949	3	4	3
46-50	392	239	806	749	691	625	200	786	739	702	645	34341	2	3	4
51-55	755	1038	1473	1272	1070	868	878	1603	1362	1120	879	61677	1	1	2
56+	1140	271	248	212	176	140	388	987	772	556	341	68794	8	2	1

Note: See Table 4.4 for explanation of measures A, B, C_i, D, E_i, and Dependence.

Source: Compiled by the authors.

TABLE 4.7

Different Measures Displayed with Respect to Salary
(average values per individual)

Salary (in pounds)	A	B	C_1	C_2	C_3	C_4	D	E_1	E_2	E_3	E_4	Dependence	C Rank	E Rank	Dependence Rank
Less than 1500	305	199	447	415	383	351	125	458	427	395	363	20334	5	5-7	10
1,501-1,750	188	167	342	314	285	260	116	364	334	304	274	30745	6-8	8	8
1,751-2,000	284	130	376	344	311	278	155	457	414	370	326	24243	6-8	5-7	9
2,001-2,250	310	116	335	309	283	258	131	313	294	275	257	30838	9	9	7
2,251-2,500	428	207	617	570	523	477	208	615	559	502	445	31115	3-4	4	6
2,501-2,750	156	102	280	252	223	195	31	230	218	205	193	31544	10	10	5
2,751-3,000	621	206	652	601	549	498	206	647	596	544	493	45159	2-3	3	3
3,001-3,250	557	540	480	395	310	225	*	*	*	*	*	37097	6-8	5-7	4
3,251-3,500	270	453	791	678	564	451	377	749	655	560	466	58581	2-4	2	2
More than 3500	463	434	1269	1160	1052	944	334	1506	1365	1225	1085	73229	1	1	1

See Table 4.4 for explanation of measures A, B, C_i, D, E_i, and Dependence.

*As not all respondents gave replies to provide A,B,D, the C_i and E_i measures only derive from respondents where both A and B or A and D replies were received.

Source: Compiled by the authors.

TABLE 4.8

Different Measures Displayed with Respect to Years Spent in Research and Development
(average values per individual)

Years in R&D	A	B	C_1	C_2	C_3	C_4	D	E_1	E_2	E_3	E_4	Dependence	C Rank	E Rank	Dependence Rank
0-5	244	183	412	376	339	297	117	448	410	372	334	27061	6	3-5	5
6-10	339	228	500	454	408	362	207	491	442	393	344	33778	4	3-5	3
11-15	477	146	512	480	448	416	82	474	453	432	411	24873	3	3-5	6
16-20	313	70	326	309	292	275	111	350	323	306	289	31366	5	6	4
21-25	539	275	850	777	704	631	204	716	669	622	575	41894	2	2	2
Over 25	692	1385	1975	1723	1471	1219	1373	2518	2113	1708	1303	103183	1	1	1

Note: See Table 4.4 for explanation of measures A, B, C_i; D, E_i, and Dependence.

Source: Compiled by the authors.

TABLE 4.9

Different Measures Displayed with Respect to Discipline
(average values per individual)

Discipline	A	B	C_1	C_2	C_3	C_4	D	E_1	E_2	E_3	E_4	Dependence	C Rank	E Rank	Dependence Rank
Chemistry	440	126	526	484	442	391	211	467	433	400	367	38089	4	3	2
Medical/biological	381	24	769	672	575	478	*	*	*	*	*	10506	2	—	10
Agriculture--animals/plants	202	82	323	293	263	209	104	270	248	225	203	26609	6	6	7
Food	620	8	58	54	50	46	10	52	49	47	45	30341	10	9	3
Textile	384	130	590	541	492	447	215	889	802	713	626	29633	3	1	4
Material—metal/metallurgy/metal finishing	126	98	226	206	185	164	83	223	200	178	155	39244	8	8	1
Physics/acoustics	123	115	216	193	170	146	86	248	217	186	154	18554	9	7	9
Mechanical engineering	458	212	710	664	618	578	195	680	631	587	533	28953	1	2	5
Electrical engineering/communications	249	135	466	423	379	335	201	470	430	389	349	22696	5	4	8
Computers/control	122	11	230	208	186	164	89	291	261	231	200	27455	7	5	6

*As not all respondents gave replies to provide A, B, D, the C_i and E_i measures only derive from respondents where both A and B or A and D replies were received.

Note. See Table 4.4 for explanation of measures A, B, C_i, D, E_i, and Dependence.

values in Table 4.6. Apart from this case, the value attached to information varies in rank order with the age of the respondents.

One immediate explanation is that salary is used to weight the number of hours and salary is correlated with age. This explanation, however, fails to take account of the variations in the time spent on research and development and the variations in the changes in that time when secondary information is withdrawn.

The index of dependence reflects less successfully the B and D values, but does correspond to the ranking of the E values, and, save for the over 55's, the C values. It is, however, only the B and D values for those between 41 and 45 years that distort the two rankings. There does not seem any simple explanation for this result.

Effectiveness Measures and Salary

At first sight it would not appear from Table 4.7 that there is any striking correlation between A values and salary. However, a moving average of the A values does indeed increase with the salary of the individual respondents. No corresponding correlation exists for the B or D values, where all that can be noted is that where salary is greater than £2,750 the values are considerably larger than for lower salaries.

There is satisfactory correspondence between the ranking of the C and E values. The slight variations in rankings within the C and E values, as a result of using different coefficients for the B and D values in their computation, are, as before, acceptable, for the variations in the absolute values are so small as to be insignificant. Dependence indexes here correspond roughly to the ranks of the C and E values and are similar to those in Table 4.6.

Effectiveness Measures and Years Spent in Research and Development

It was considered that different results might emerge as a function of the number of years spent in R & D work. Table 4.8 indicates, however, considerable similarity between these classifications. In Tables 4.6 and 4.8 we find essentially the same rankings.

Effectiveness Measures and Respondent's Discipline

The next stratification of the respondents' results comes from their discipline groupings. Table 4.9 shows acceptably similar rankings for the C and E values.

TABLE 4.10

Aggregate Effectiveness Values per Industry

Industry	Effectiveness Measure per Industry (hundreds)									Dependence Index	Ranking							Total Number of R & D Workers
	A	B	C_1	C_2	C_3	C_4	D	E_1	E_2	E_3	E_4		A	B	C_1	D	E_1	Dependence Index	
Agriculture	5751	2891	5711	5162	4614	4062	1321	4419	4124	3832	3538	429	5	5	5	5	5	5	5
Aircraft	25600	32082	44126	38885	33621	28349	44936	43170	38840	34519	30163	9941	2	2	2	1	2	2	2
Chemicals	19704	8459	14584	13185	11780	10375	7188	15938	14526	13118	11707	9790	3	3	3	3	3	3	3
Electrical engineering	41638	39282	66947	61171	55396	49588	25571	48842	43281	37715	32144	37133	1	1	1	2	1	1	1
Textiles	9243	5623	14443	13253	12067	10877	6751	14438	12919	11403	9784	4535	4	4	4	4	4	4	4

Note: See Table 4.4 for explanation of measures A, B, C_i, D, E_i, and Dependence.

Source: Compiled by the authors.

TABLE 4.11

Average Effectiveness Values per Firm in Each Industry

Industry	Effectiveness Measure per Firm (hundreds)											Dependence Index	Ranking					
	A	B	C_1	C_2	C_3	C_4	D	E_1	E_2	E_3	E_4		A	B	C_1	D	E_1	Dependence Index
Agriculture	174	88	173	156	140	123	40	134	125	116	107	13	3	3	3	3	3	5
Aircraft	337	422	581	512	442	373	591	568	511	454	397	131	1	1	1	1	1	2
Chemicals	79	34	58	53	47	42	29	64	58	52	46	39	4	4	4	4	4	3
Electrical engineering	186	175	299	273	247	221	114	218	193	168	143	166	2	2	2	2	2	1
Textiles	37	23	58	53	49	44	27	58	52	46	40	18	5	5	5	5	5	4
All	123	106	175	158	141	124	103	153	137	121	105	74						

Note: See Table 4.4 for explanation of measures A, B, C_i, D, E_i, and Dependence.

Source: Compiled by the authors.

Since the number of respondents in each discipline group is fairly small, the variations in ranking are less satisfactory than in other instances. It is worth recalling that while the electrical engineering industry gave relatively lower marks to published secondary information than other sources of such information, electrical engineers give a value to the published information that places them centrally in the range of disciplinary value.

Textile technologists, chemists, and mechanical engineers obtain most value from secondary information, while metallurgists appear most dependent upon it.

BREAKDOWN BY INDUSTRY AND TYPE OF SERVICE

In Table 4.10 the values are given as totals for the industries, grossed up to take account of the sampling procedures. An inspection of the results in Table 4.10 indicates the following points:

1. The section of the table that ranks each industry by the value placed on secondary information services (the highest value being represented by a ranking of 1 and the lowest by a ranking of 5) suggests that of the five industries, agriculture places the lowest value on secondary information services. The textile industry has a ranking of 4. The chemical industry is given a rank of 3 by the majority of the measures, although with regard to the C measures there is only a marginal difference between chemicals and textiles. While the chemical industry appears to be more dependent on secondary information than the aircraft industry, the latter comfortably achieves a ranking of 2. Topping the list is the electrical engineering industry, which with one exception places the highest value on secondary information services.

2. The A values exceed the B and D values.

3. The sensitivity to the coefficients applied in the calculation of the C values is illustrated when the values for the chemical and textile industries are compared. In the case of C_1 a marginally higher value is given by the chemical industry, while the reverse is true for C_2, C_3, and C_4.

4. If we compare $(A + B)$ with the C measures and $(A + D)$ with the E measures it will be seen that the aircraft, chemicals, and electrical engineering industries place by implication considerable value on the internally provided services, while the agriculture and textiles industries appear to place a relatively low value on such services. This does not influence the ranking of relative values placed on secondary information by each industry.

5. The final column in Table 4.10 ranks the R & D work force in terms of size. A comparison of the value ranking and the ranking of the R & D work force shows that the aircraft and electrical engineering industries are placed at the top and that agriculture and textiles fall into the lowest positions in both series. This would seem to support a hypothesis that the values placed on secondary information by

each industry are determined by the number of R & D workers employed in each industry.

In order to eliminate the influence of size on the effectiveness values placed on secondary information services, these values have been deflated in Table 4.11 by the number of firms engaging in R & D work in each industry, and in Table 4.12 by the number of R & D workers in each industry.

The following points emerge from an examination of Table 4.11:

1. The ranking of individual measures of value by each industry maintains certain consistency. Perhaps the most significant change from the results appearing in Table 4.10 is that agriculture moves up to third place. Once again the aircraft and electrical engineering industries take the top positions, although in reverse order. The advance of agriculture has pushed chemicals and textiles into the bottom two positions.

2. The low Dependence Index given by agriculture contrasts with the relatively high evaluation reflected by the other measures. This may suggest that satisfactory alternative sources of information are more easily available to the agriculture industry.

The results in Table 4.12 are expressed in terms of the average value placed on secondary information services by the individual R & D worker in each industry. Points that may be noted include the following:

1. The relative value that each industry places on secondary information services has changed significantly from Table 4.11 to Table 4.12. The ranking of the different measures indicates that the individual R & D worker in the textile industry assigns the highest value to secondary information. Aircraft drops to bottom place, being placed fifth by four out of the six ranked measures. The values of the other three industries, and in particular the chemicals industry, fluctuate and overall there would appear to be little to choose between them, although since agriculture is placed third and electrical engineering fourth by three out of the six measures, this suggests that chemicals by virtue of being placed first by two measures and second by one might take second place.

2. The very low Dependence measures given by aircraft and agriculture, which differ only marginally, contrast with the relatively higher values given by the other measures in the agriculture as opposed to the aircraft industry.

3. The deflation of the measures by the number of R & D workers in each industry has significantly altered the ranking and it would appear, perhaps not surprisingly, that this factor will tend to determine the aggregate value an industry places on secondary information. This is an important consideration in view of the conclusion drawn from Table 4.10 that the aircraft and electrical engineering industries have the highest aggregate values. Although they appear to fall in the fourth and fifth positions as far as average value per R & D worker

TABLE 4.12

Average Effectiveness Values per Individual in Each Industry

Industry	Effectiveness Measures per Individual (hundreds)										Dependence Index	Ranking					Dependence Index
	A	B	C_1	C_2	C_3	C_4	D	E_1	E_2	E_3	E_4		A	B	C_1	D	E_1	
Agriculture	3.9	2.0	3.9	3.5	3.2	2.8	0.9	3.0	2.8	2.6	2.4	0.3	3	4	2	5	4	5
Aircraft	2.1	2.6	3.6	3.2	2.8	2.3	3.7	3.5	3.2	2.8	2.5	0.8	5	2	4	1	3	4
Chemicals	4.7	2.0	3.4	3.1	2.8	2.5	1.7	3.8	3.4	3.1	2.8	2.3	1	4	5	3	2	1
Electrical engineering	2.3	2.2	3.7	3.4	3.1	2.8	1.4	2.7	2.4	2.1	1.8	2.1	4	3	3	4	5	3
Textiles	4.4	2.7	6.9	6.4	5.8	5.2	3.2	6.9	6.2	5.5	4.7	2.2	2	1	1	2	1	2
All	2.7	2.3	3.8	3.4	3.1	2.7	2.2	3.3	3.0	2.6	2.3	1.6						

Note: See Table 4.4 for explanation of measures A, B, C_1, D, E_1, and Dependence.

Source: Compiled by the authors.

is concerned, it seems likely that, for a given investment in secondary information, these two industries probably would receive the greatest benefit, purely on the basis that they have a considerably larger R & D work force than the other three industries.

While we may conclude that aggregate values are largely determined by the size of the R & D work force, this does not explain why the average measures of value per individual R & D worker in each industry differ. There are variations between firms within an industry as well as between industries. In addition, it seems probable that an individual evaluation of the effectiveness of secondary information services will depend partly on the type of service that is used and partly on the characteristics of one service as compared to those of another. A further factor is likely to be the information needs that the individual user requires a given service to satisfy. For example, a person with a need for current awareness only may well evaluate a given service in rather different terms from a person who has only an information retrieval need. The following tables have been designed to investigate whether any of these factors do influence the effectiveness value placed on secondary information services.

The sampling procedure that was adopted for the field survey was stratified. From the population, firms that possessed the largest stocks of current periodicals were selected for each industry. These firms might be broadly described as being "information-conscious" (I-C). The remainder of the sample was selected randomly from a population of firms in each industry with no regard as to the size of their stocks of current periodicals, and for purposes of differentiating them from "information-conscious" firms we shall describe them as "other" (O). The average effectiveness values per firm in the group of I-C firms have been calculated and compared with the corresponding values for the group of O firms and the results are shown in Table 4.13.

Across all industries, the results in Table 4.13 suggest that I-C firms place a significantly higher value on secondary information than O firms. When these results are examined by individual industries, we find that it is only in the electrical engineering industry that the average I-C firm values are not significantly greater than corresponding O firm values. Insofar as a high value will represent a high demand for secondary information services, we might conclude from these results that the supply of technical information creates it own demand.

A similar classification of the different effectiveness values by I-C and O firms in each industry and across the five industries is given in Table 4.14, but this time the different measures are expressed in terms of average value per individual rather than per firm. Those results, although possessing smaller variance, indicate that the average individual R & D worker in the I-C firms places a higher value on secondary information than his counterpart in the O firms.

TABLE 4.13

Average Effectiveness Values per Firm
Classified by Information-Conscious
and Other Firms, between Industries

Industry	Type of Firm	Effectiveness Measures per Firm					Dependence Index
		A	B	C_1	D	E_1	
Agriculture	I-C	631	443	918	206	724	562
	O	73	9	8	3	3	34
Aircraft	I-C	1755	4050	4465	6019	4104	629
	O	215	111	248	126	265	88
Chemicals	I-C	2216	1061	1036	600	1002	837
	O	35	13	38	15	45	23
Electrical engineering	I-C	420	168	135	159	122	119
	O	179	176	303	113	221	167
Textiles	I-C	873	639	1502	873	1547	361
	O	17	7	43	6	21	10
All	I-C	1143	1279	1323	1625	1234	447
	O	86	64	123	48	103	64

Note: See Table 4.4 for explanation of measures A, B, C_i, D, E_i, and Dependence.

Source: Compiled by the authors.

Apart from the pairs of A measures of effectiveness given by agriculture and aircraft, which are alien to the general trend, the striking exception is once again the electrical engineering industry where the reverse tendency operates in five of the six measures of value given. Why this should be the case is not immediately clear although it is possible that I-C and O firms are both well supplied with external secondary information services, and the fact that the I-C firms have large stocks of current periodicals that provide easily accessible alternative sources of information means that the O firms are more dependent on secondary information and as a result regard it more highly. If this is the case it might be that the available supply of secondary information services is likely to be of greatest importance.

A further factor that might be of influence in determining the value of secondary information services is the type of service provided and used. The total quantity of secondary information and its quality may exert influence on the effectiveness value placed on secondary information services. For example, there might be a qualitative difference if all information was provided in the form of titles lists, on the one hand, or publications containing only abstracts, on the other.

An attempt has been made to take account of this qualitative factor in Tables 4.15 and 4.16 in which the various average individual values of effectiveness are classified by type of service across industry (Table 4.15) and between I-C and O firms within each industry (Table 4.16).

Inspection of the results in Table 4.15 yields these conclusions:

1. The average R & D worker considers "pure abstracts" to be an overwhelmingly superior method of presenting secondary information than any of the other services that are available to him.

2. The rankings of the different effectiveness measures consistently evaluate pure abstracts most highly, while enquiry answering (EA) services and "other"* are given the lowest values. There appears to be little to choose between the other three types of service.

3. The values given are overall values, and it is conceded that a titles list that is generally designed specifically for current awareness (CA) might possibly receive a higher value for satisfying a CA need than say a pure abstract publication that is not designed solely to satisfy that need for information. This point is considered in Table 4.17 where an evaluation for each type of service is made separately for CA needs and for information retrieval (IR) needs.

4. Despite the tendency for Selective Dissemination of Information services (SDI) to be tailored to meet the needs of the information user, this type of service receives a low value. The low effectiveness rating of SDI services must be interpreted with some caution because these figures are based on the assumption that firms or individual R & D workers who do not make use of such services attach a zero value to them. The fact that there were never more than four observations obtained in a given I-C or O category within each industry in respect to SDI services indicates that use of this type of service is not widespread.

5. It should be remembered that these different types of service are not complete substitutes for each other and that, although the results indicate there is a decided preference for pure abstracts, this does not necessarily mean that all the other services should no longer be produced.

The classification of average individual effectiveness values by type of service and by I-C and O firms within each industry is combined in Table 4.16. An explanation of the results in this table should give some indication whether these factors offer an explanation for

---

*The services included in "other" were those that provided information on standards, specifications, etc.

TABLE 4.14

Average Effectiveness
Values per Individual in Information-Conscious
and Other Firms, by Industry

		Effectiveness Measures per Individual					Dependence Index
Industry	Type of Firm	A	B	C_1	D	E_1	
Agriculture	I-C	3.5	2.5	5.1	1.2	4.0	3.1
	O	5.1	0.6	0.5	0.2	0.2	2.4
Aircraft	I-C	1.6	3.6	4.0	5.4	3.6	5.6
	O	2.8	1.4	3.2	1.6	3.4	11.2
Chemicals	I-C	8.3	4.0	3.9	2.7	3.7	3.1
	O	3.0	1.1	3.2	1.2	3.8	1.9
Electrical engineering	I-C	2.4	1.0	0.8	0.9	0.7	0.7
	O	2.3	2.3	3.9	1.5	2.9	2.2
Textiles	I-C	6.0	4.4	10.3	6.0	10.6	2.5
	O	3.3	1.5	8.6	1.3	4.2	2.0
All	I-C	3.3	3.3	4.3	4.0	4.0	1.5
	O	2.6	1.8	3.6	1.5	3.1	1.9

Note: See Table 4.4 for explanation of measures A, B, C_i, D, E_i, and Dependence.

Source: Compiled by the authors.

variation in the evaluation of secondary information within and between industries.

Although there are not an acceptable number of observations to support significantly each unit value given in the table (those values that are derived from less than five observations are indicated in the tables by an asterisk), these points may be made:

1. The general picture in the figures in Table 4.15 whereby pure abstracts were seen to be most effective is broadly reproduced in Table 4.16. In the electrical engineering and aircraft industries, pure abstracts are placed well ahead by each of the different measures. This is true also of the I-C firms in the chemical and textile industries. The exception among the I-C firms is in agriculture in which the I-C firms, although placing pure abstracts at the top of the list in the C and E values, regard titles lists as meriting some consideration. Similarly the O firms in the chemicals industry look upon abstracts

TABLE 4.15

Average Effectiveness Values per Individual
by Type of Service and Ranking of Selected Measures

Type of Service	Effectiveness Measures per Individual								Ranking		
	C_1	C_2	C_3	C_4	E_1	E_2	E_3	E_4	Dependence Index	C_1	E_1	Dependence Index
Titles lists	33	30	27	24	34	31	28	25	15	2	2	3
Pure abstracts	268	242	216	190	208	188	166	144	120	1	1	1
Abstracts in primary publications	31	28	26	23	33	30	26	23	18	3	3	2
Selective dissemination of information services (SDI)	29	26	23	20	33	29	25	21	10	4	3	4
Enquiry answering services (EA)	8	7	6	5	8	7	6	5	7	5	5	5
Other	4	4	3	3	5	5	4	4	2	6	6	6

Note: See Table 4.4 for explanation of measures A, B, C_i, D, E_i, and Dependence.

Source: Compiled by the authors.

TABLE 4.16

Average Effectiveness Values per Individual
by Type of Service in Information-Conscious
and Other Firms, by Industry

Industry	Type of Firm	Type of Service	Effectiveness Measures Per Individual								Dependence Index
			C_1	C_2	C_3	C_4	E_1	E_2	E_3	E_4	
Agriculture	I-C	Titles lists	151	137	123	109	127	115	104	92	129
		Pure abstracts	292	269	247	224	239	228	216	205	136
		Abstracts in primary journals	68	55	43	31	36	32	28	24	33
		SDI service	0	0	0	0	0	0	0	0	15
		EA service	1	1	1	1	2	2	2	2	1
	O	Titles lists	0	0	0	0	0	0	0	0	0
		Pure abstracts	40	36	32	28	8	8	7	7	57
		Abstracts in primary journals	8	8	8	7	6	6	6	5	180
		EA Service	5	5	5	5	5	5	5	5	4
Chemicals	I-C	Titles lists	54	52	49	47	56	53	50	47	41
		Pure abstracts	230	205	179	153	230	208	186	164	185
		Abstracts in primary journals	62	60	58	56	62	60	57	55	70
		SDI service	39	32	26	19	26	23	20	17	15
	O	Titles lists	1	1	1	1	1	1	1	1	2
		Pure abstracts	156	141	126	111	163	148	134	120	103
		Abstracts in journals	129	117	106	94	175	158	142	126	57
		SDI service	29	25	21	17	29	25	21	18	24
		EA service	3	3	3	3	3	3	3	3	3
		Other	8	7	6	5	8	7	6	5	4
Aircraft	I-C	Titles lists	4	3	2	1	4	3	2	1	6
		Pure abstracts	383	332	280	229	360	326	291	257	43
		Abstracts in primary journals	10	8	7	5	0	0	0	0	7

Industry	Type of Firm	Type of Service	Effectiveness Measures Per Individual								Dependence Index
			C_1	C_2	C_3	C_4	E_1	E_2	E_3	E_4	
Aircraft	O	Titles lists	35	32	29	26	35	32	29	26	10
		Pure abstracts	187	169	151	133	198	178	157	136	64
		Abstracts in primary journals	41	37	33	29	52	45	38	31	13
		SDI service	21	21	21	21	21	21	21	21	4
		EA service	31	26	22	17	31	26	22	17	20
		Other	0	0	0	0	0	0	0	0	1
Electrical engineering	I-C	Titles lists	10	8	7	5	7	6	5	4	8
		Pure abstracts	58	53	48	43	54	50	46	42	59
		Abstracts in primary journals	1	1	1	1	1	1	1	1	0
		Other	8	7	7	6	8	7	7	6	1
	O	Titles lists	44	41	37	33	49	44	40	35	15
		Pure abstracts	293	269	244	219	171	151	131	111	174
		Abstracts in primary journals	6	6	5	5	7	6	6	5	7
		SDI service	39	35	30	26	48	42	35	29	10
		EA service	5	4	4	3	5	5	4	3	9
		Other	3	3	2	2	4	3	3	3	1
Textiles	I-C	Titles lists	8	8	7	7	12	12	12	12	4
		Pure abstracts	938	852	765	678	942	820	701	583	221
	O	Titles lists	21	20	20	19	21	20	20	19	12
		Pure abstracts	46	41	37	32	45	40	36	32	36
		Abstracts in primary journals	160	148	135	122	95	87	79	70	43
		SDI service	144	133	121	110	153	139	126	112	70
		EA service	29	27	25	24	28	27	25	24	8
		Other	49	46	43	40	84	78	72	66	27

Note: See Table 4.4 for explanation of measures A, B, C_i, D, E_i, & Dependence.

Source: Compiled by the authors.

contained in primary journals as second to pure abstracts. Only the O firms in the textile industry do not give pure abstracts the highest value. In the Dependence Index and E values, they regard SDI most highly with abstracts contained in primary journals falling not too far behind, while the C values place the latter type of service slightly ahead of the former. Pure abstracts are assigned a very low relative mark.

2. The position observed in Table 4.13 that I-C firms give a higher value to secondary information than O firms is repeated, again with the exception of the electrical engineering industry.

3. The range of positively valued secondary information services that are made use of by O firms exceeds that of I-C firms in every industry except the agricultural industry. This may be a reflection of a tendency for O firms to be smaller in size than the I-C firms and for small firms to undertake greater specialization in production and research activities.

The results in Tables 4.15 and 4.16 indicate that pure abstracts are usually considered the most effective type of secondary information service. As a check on these results on analysis was made of the characteristics possessed by secondary information services. This was done by identifying the characteristics that respondents considered to be important, obtaining the relative degree of importance of these characteristics, and ascertaining how satisfied the respondents were in respect to each characteristic for each type of service. Satisfaction and importance were combined and weighted. What these values attempt to measure is the relative effectiveness of a given type of service in respect to a particular characteristic. In Table 4.17, for example, we find that titles lists give greater value or satisfaction for the coverage characteristic than for speed.

Points of note that emerge from the results given in Table 4.17 include the following:

1. Pure abstracts receive the highest characteristic mark of all types of service for speed and coverage, and indeed for each of the characteristics identified as being important by respondents.

2. The characteristic of pure abstracts that achieves the highest evaluation is relevance, and this may be rather surprising. However, if this result is taken in conjunction with the high value placed on the arrangement characteristic, the explanation may be that with a satisfactory subject arrangement problems of irrelevant material are considerably reduced.

3. The relatively low value assigned to the pure abstracts indexing characteristic suggests that even if pure abstracts are used for retrieval purposes the information user will tend to obtain the relevant information via the arrangement rather than through the index. This may reflect the suspicion that although the index will direct attention to what are prima facie relevant items, it will also lead one to a number of irrelevant items and at the same time may cause the loss of some relevant items. The fear of the latter and the resulting

TABLE 4.17

Average Characteristic Effectiveness Values
per Individual by Type of Service

Type of Service	Characteristics								Characteristic Values by Information Need	
	Speed	Coverage	Relevance	Detail	Arrangement	Indexing	Additional Services		Current Awareness	Information Retrieval
Titles lists	2	5	2	2	4	2	0		10	6
Pure abstracts	22	79	119	49	64	8	22		31	23
Abstracts in primary publications	2	6	3	4	2	1	0		8	5
SDI	3	2	2	2	1	0	0		3	2
MA	4	1	1	1	1	3	8		1	3
Other	0	0	0	0	0	0	0		1	1

Note: See Table 4.4 for explanation of measures A, B, C_i, D, E_i, and Dependence.

Source: Compiled by the authors.

lack of confidence in the reliability of the index to give adequate coverage may explain the high value placed on arrangement.

4. A similar explanation may underlie the coverage characteristic receiving only half the value obtained by speed, relevance, and detail. The suspicion may exist that a number of items may have been omitted that would have been relevant.

5. The reletively high mark given for the additional services characteristic with respect to enquiry answering confirms the value of back-up services, that is, the provision of the material referred to. The significance of the even higher value given to pure abstracts for the same characteristic is less obvious.

6. It may be argued that a titles list is primarily designed to be a current awareness tool and that to compare it with, say, pure abstracts, which are designed to serve retrieval needs, may be misleading. It may indeed be the case that for a current awareness need titles lists will achieve greater effectiveness than any other type of service.

In order to test this argument, the information needs of the R & D worker were divided into two classes—current awareness (CA) and information retrieval (IR)—and effectiveness values were obtained in respect to each characteristic for each of these two classes. Comparable aggregate characteristic values of effectiveness were then obtained for each of the CA and IR classes. These values for each type of service appear in the two right-hand columns of Table 4.17. The evidence points to pure abstracts being more effective for each type of need than any other service. For a CA information need, titles lists fall into second place some considerable way below pure abstracts. It is of interest to note that pure abstracts are more highly valued as a CA tool than for their ability to satisfy IR needs.

The foregoing results are intended to illustrate a methodology, but certain conclusions may tentatively be drawn from these results:

1. The number of R & D personnel, as defined earlier in this study, largely determines the aggregate value of secondary information services in a given industry.

2. Two factors of considerable importance in explaining differences in the per capita value assigned to secondary information appear to be the supply of technical information that is available and the type of service by which secondary information is disseminated.

3. Pure abstracts are considered to be generally the most effective means of satisfying the respective current awareness and information retrieval needs of the R & D worker. Some reservation, however, must be placed on the low values assigned to SDI services because of the small number of observations.

ANALYSIS OF COST RESULTS

The figures obtained for the costs of producing secondary information are based on the detailed costing studies performed according to the procedure set out in Appendix C. Fourteen studies were carried out in detail and a further three information systems were visited and partial studies were performed and an estimated of the total cost of each was made.

The 17 information systems between them provided the following number of services: abstracts journals—15; SDI—5; enquiry answering—11. Not all systems provide the three services together, and in fact only three of all the information systems did so. It could be hypothesized that it is more efficient to run all three services together, but there is not enough evidence available to produce a statistically valid conclusion on this point.

A striking feature of the secondary information field is the small size of the production unit. The average yearly cost of the system investigated was £26,000 and the size distribution of expenditure on the individual services is hown in Table 4.18.

Not only is the average size quite small, but there appears to be a large number at the lower end of the scale with an annual budget of less than £15,000. The size of the enquiry answering and SDI services may increase in the future. There are various reasons for the present small size, probably the most important being the extent of the subject field that is served and thus the only way the size of the units could be increased would be to amalgamate systems across subject fields. This would involve in many cases the bringing together of different specialities that come under the same subject field; however, the question of gains from larger-scale output is somewhat problematical and it is difficult to generalize with a great degree of certainty.

United Kingdom Expenditure on Secondary Information Systems

It is possible to generalize to some extent from the results obtained and calculate the total cost of secondary information systems in the United Kingdom in this context. Our investigations suggest that there are between 135 and 160 information systems in the United Kingdom, and on the basis of this it is possible to gross up the current total cost of the systems analyzed, which amounted to £440,000 according to the fractions 135/17 and 160/17 to give a rough and ready idea of the total expenditure; this appears to be in the range of £3.5 million to £4.1 million per annum. It should be noted that expenditures within firms are not included in this and it by no means represents the total cost of secondary information to the country as a whole, particularly as several expensive services are purchased from abroad. Furthermore, the systems costed were not chosen on a strictly random basis and the generalization on total expenditure should be regarded only as an order of magnitude rather than as an exact figure.

TABLE 4.18

Information Systems: Size Distribution

Annual Cost (in pounds)	Systems	Abstracts	Number of Services Enquiry Answering	SDI
Less than 15,000	6	5	11	4
16,000-25,000	2	2		1
26,000-35,000	5	5		
36,000-45,000	2	2		
More than 46,000	2	1		

Source: Compiled by the authors.

Costs in Detail

In each costing study an attempt was made to break down the costs according to the classifications developed earlier, and the result of performing this operation on each of 15 abstracting services is shown in Table 4.19.

These costs are in index form to ensure confidentiality, but are nonetheless in a form that makes them comparable with each other. Under the "Cost per Abstract" heading the manpower costs of producing abstracts have been divided by the number of abstracts produced to give a cost per abstract, and this figure has been multiplied by an index factor. The total manpower cost per abstract is under the appropriate heading, while the "Grand Total" refers to the cost per abstract including all costs such as printing, distribution, etc.

In a similar manner the cost per subscriber has been obtained by dividing the printing, distribution, and total costs by the number of subscribers and multiplying by the same index factor.

The bottom row shows the index of quality used, which was the average number of words per abstract exclusive of bibliographical details.

As may be observed, the attempt at a breakdown of costs was reasonably successful, a full breakdown having been achieved in six cases and an informative breakdown in another six. An important point regarding this table is that not all of these services produce abstracts as such, that is, some provide indexes or classified lists and thus receive a zero index of length and have no costs entered under the "Abstracting" heading. Furthermore, there is no single classification of costs that is consistently large enough to influence the cost per abstract in terms of manpower cost. Thus it is not

TABLE 4.19

Production of Abstracts—Costs in Index Form

Services	1	2	3	4	5	6	7	8	9	10	11	12	13	14	15
								Cost per Abstract							
Scanning	89	20	540	589	36	81	786		*			4	*	*	
Abstracting	480	161	448	3000	508	173		444	56*	32	262	4	266*	101	
Indexing	77	89	97	302	65		145		28			85	16	12	
Editing	173	351	181	77	133	48	169		36			28	*	97*	
Proofreading	133		32	65	32		52							*	
Miscellaneous professional							77		4			28			
Clerical	133	97	105	169	73	77	105	52	32	4	12	44	28	24	
Management	145	93	266	306	105	60	28		8	4		48	20	24	
Total manpower cost	1226	810	1669	5214	1000	468	1367	496	165	40	274	242	327	258	1004
Grand total	2137	1867	5069	10056	1524	988	1835	945	512	197	351	544	806	1149	
								Cost per Subscriber							
Printing	2226	819	270	1613	1802	1004	1601	1331	3577	2008	6056	3702	5690		
Distribution	177	141	282	133	**	117	**	383	1024	202	69	258			
Grand total	7609	2145	690	6323	6754	2133	8964	3899	8907	3391	28577	7895	11355		
Index	129	101	78	390	93	86	74	50	0	0	40	0	61	100	41

*Included together.
**No figure available.

Source: Compiled by the authors.

immediately clear why the cost per abstract in terms of manpower only should vary so remarkably from an index of 40 to 5214. A great deal of information on the qualitative aspects of the information systems costed was collected on the basis of the noncost section of Appendix C and it was assumed that the qualitative aspects would have some effect on the cost per abstract, particularly in terms of manpower. However, this information was so diverse in its nature that it did not lend itself to use in statistical analysis and a rather different approach was adopted.

The Cost of an Abstract

From inspection it appeared that the cost per abstract in manpower terms varied with the length of the abstract produced, and an index of length was prepared for each service by selecting a large random sample of the output of each system and calculating the average length of words per abstract exclusive of bibliographical details. This index of length was regarded as an index of the quality of the services and thus there is no value judgment involved in the determination of the quality of the output—for example, whether it is "indicative" or "informative," or whether it is indexed monthly, yearly, or five yearly. The qualitative factors arising within the system such as the qualifications and experience of the abstracting staff are also ignored.

A further aspect of production that is generally held by economists to affect the cost per unit is the scale of output, the normal postulate being that the larger the number of items produced the lower the unit costs. This phenomenon is referred to as increasing returns and the effect of this upon unit costs will also be tested.

The basic model suggested here that seems likely to explain the variation in the cost per abstract is therefore:

$$C = F(I, O)$$

where C = total manpower cost per abstract
I = index of length
O = number of items of output.

A method of refining this model is to subtract the cost of management from the unit cost calculations, and to use the model

$$C_1 = F(I_1, O)$$

where C_1 = manpower cost per abstract net of management

The effect of increasing returns can be investigated more explicitly by using the following model:

$$\frac{C}{I} = F(O)$$

This model will show the effect of the scale of output on the "cost per word," but because some systems have a zero index of length it is necessary to drop three observations. (Another slight problem relating to the data is that the costings were not all performed for the same year, and all costs were standardized to the same year by using the index of wages and salaries in the Annual Abstract of Statistics.)

The first step here is to examine the correlation coefficients between the dependent variables C, C_1, and C/I and the explanatory variables I, O, and I/O:

	I	O
C	.938	-.382
C_1	.938	-.395
$\frac{C}{I}$	—	-.301

It is apparent that there is a very strong relationship between the cost per abstract and the index of length. It is to be expected that some relationship would exist here but it is surprising to find a relationship of such strength, particularly when so many influences have not been taken into account. There does not appear to be a significant relationship between the cost per abstract and the scale of output, even when the variable C/I is used, although the correlation coefficients do have the expected negative sign that reflects the tendency toward an inverse relationship between the two. It is interesting to note that the use of C_1 as a dependent variable does not materially affect the results.

The estimated regression model is shown in Table 4.20, where in the case of the first model the variables are regressed singly in cases 1 and 2 and then together in case 3.

The figures in parentheses below the regression coefficients refer to the "t" value, which is significant at the 1 percent level for values greater than 2.6.

It is clear that I is the main variable in explaining variation in cost per abstract, while O explains very little on its own in terms of R^2 and the regression coefficient is only significant at the 20 percent level. When I and O are combined in the multiple regression (see regression 3 in Table 4.20) then the coefficient of O is not statistically different from zero and in fact detracts from the value of the R^{-2} obtained from using I on its own. Inspection of regression 4 also reveals that the effect of increasing returns is not significant, although the regression coefficient does have the expected negative sign.

The main point arising from this analysis is that the length of the abstract on its own accounts for 87 percent of the variation in the cost per abstract. This means that the main qualitative considerations

TABLE 4.20

The Relationship Between Cost per Abstract
and Index of Length and Number Produced

Regression number	Dependent variable	Constant	I	O	R^2	R^{-2}
1	C	-23	3.160 (9.8)		.8798	.8706
	C_1	-10	2.725 (9.8)		.8807	.8715
2	C	338		-.086 (1.5)	.1457	.0800
	C_1	304		-.077 (1.6)	.1563	.0914
3	C	-30	3.186 (8.6)	.004 (0.2)	.8801	.8601
	C_1	-11	2.729 (8.5)	.0005 (0.02)	.8807	.8608
4	$\frac{C}{I}$	313		-59.706 (1.0)	.0904	.0000

Source: Compiled by the authors.

in abstracts costs arises from an examination of the length of abstract produced.

Amalgamation of Secondary Information Systems

It can be argued that certain economies of scale would arise on amalgamation, particularly with respect to printing and distribution; the zero-order correlation between the number of subscribers and the printing and distribution cost per subscriber is -.5, which means that the number of subscribers only accounts for 25 percent of the variation in this cost, which is itself usually less than 50 percent of the total cost of the information system.

However, the diversity of the products is such that it is unlikely that the simple correlation analysis could detect any significant relationship; for example, some services are produced monthly, and others quarterly, while there are great differences in the length of each volume. It is therefore necessary to consider the implications of amalgamation on an a priori basis.

It can be argued that there is a potential saving to be gained from amalgamations because of overlap in the services produced. In the first instance there may be overlap in the material covered in different abstract services and amalgamation could save money by eliminating this. Secondly, any overlap in subscription lists would be eliminated and a further saving would arise in respect of distribution costs. However, there are certain costs that are likely to increase rather than decrease as a result of amalgamation, the most important of these being printing costs. To take a simple example, the result of an amalgamation may be to produce a 200-page volume for 2,000 subscribers instead of two 100-page volumes for 1,000 subscribers each; doubling the length of the volume would approximately double its printing costs. The cost of a 2,000-copy printing might be about 50 percent greater than the cost of a 1,000-copy printing. Thus the result of amalgamating two such services would be to increase printing costs significantly, perhaps by as much as 50 percent, and therefore the savings associated with overlap considerations indicated above would have to be big enough to make up for this additional printing cost to make amalgamation desirable. As printing costs alone can be over 50 percent of total costs, the reduction in other costs would need to be substantial—perhaps 25 percent or more to make amalgamations viable. Nevertheless, a detailed examination of the subscription lists of abstracts journals might reveal important possibilities for economizing in the provision of secondary information. Total savings of perhaps £1 million per annum might be available if the number of U.K. abstracts journals were reduced by half.

Overhead Costs

A final point of interest here is the determination of overhead costs, which generally present the most perplexing of problems. The costs included in this category are management, rent, rates, heat, light, and office expenditure, which amount to 12 percent of the total costs collected, and thus any degree of error that arises in the cost estimates as a result of poor specification of the overhead element is likely to be small.

COST-EFFECTIVENESS MEASURES

Our intention here is to examine the extent to which the results of the cost and effectiveness studies can be combined into a cost-effectiveness relationship for secondary information systems.

The number of effectiveness observations is small in respect to some of the services examined. If, for example, only two firms out of the twenty in an industry sample gave a value for a particular service, it will be assumed that two in twenty of all firms in the industry will do so. Only the services for which two or more effectiveness observations occurred in the sample were included in the cost-effectiveness analysis. Twelve cases occurred for which costings had been performed on the services and more than two effectiveness observations occurred. Only the costs of secondary information services were considered and no account was taken of the cost of technical information systems involved.

Three of the effectiveness measures were used in this analysis, the C and E values and the dependence index of value. Aggregate values for these three were found for each of twelve services and the result of carrying out this operation is shown in Table 4.21.

The services are listed as letters of the alphabet, to ensure confidentiality, and are ranked under the appropriate headings. There would be little change in the effectiveness rankings by using C_2, C_3, C_4 and E_2, E_3, E_4 instead of C_1 and E_1, and therefore only the values C_1, E_1 and the Dependence Index will be considered in the following discussion.

The rank order is fairly similar for the C_1 and E_1 measures, but some significant differences occur between these and the Dependence Index. The three alternative measures of value give somewhat conflicting results, particularly at the top of the table. The next stop is to weight the effectiveness measures by the cost of each service, and the result of this calculation is shown in Table 4.22.

This table may be compared with Table 4.21 to assess the effects of incorporating costs into the analysis. In Table 4.22, services E, H, and B come out consistently higher in the case of all three measures of value; the alternative measures of value give more consistent results for the cost-effectiveness measure than for the effectiveness measure alone. E is the "most cost-effective" service and I the "least cost-effective."

The fact that the ranking of the services is changed so much by the inclusion of costs suggests at first glance that decisions cannot be properly made on allocating resources without consideration of costs. It could be hypothesized that cost-effectiveness is basically a function of effectiveness, that is,

$$CE = f(E)$$

where CE = cost-effectiveness
      E = effectiveness

An alternative hypothesis is that cost-effectiveness is basically a function of costs, that is,

$$CE = f(C)$$

where CE = cost-effectiveness
      C = cost

TABLE 4.21

Aggregate Effectiveness Values

Service	C Values Aggregated by Service			
	C_1	C_2	C_3	C_4
C	231	198	182	215
A	215	195	185	205
H	158	150	146	154
E }	133	104	90	119
B }	133	110	98	122
K	93	82	76	88
J	89	84	81	87
L	41	25	17	33
G	11	9	8	10
I	8	7	6	7
D	2	2	2	2
F	1	1	1	1

Service	E Values Aggregated by Service			
	E_1	E_2	E_3	E_4
C	231	198	182	215
A	226	214	208	220
H	156	149	146	153
B	139	105	88	122
J	135	111	99	123
E	133	104	90	119
K	90	80	75	85
G }	14	11	10	13
I }	14	14	14	14
L	12	11	10	11
F	5	4	4	4
D	2	2	2	2

Service	Dependence Index Aggregated and Ranked
B	5651
E	5242
C	4759
K	4535
J	4053
A	3940
L	3333
H	2694
G	1722
F	517
D	316
I	147

Source: Compiled by the authors.

TABLE 4.22

Aggregated C_1, E_1, and Dependence Index
Weighted by Cost of Service and Ranked

Service	C_1	Service	E_1	Service	Dependence Index
E	417	E	417	E	1642
H	146	H	145	B	343
B	81	B	84	H	249
C	69	C	69	L	222
A	60	A	63	K	174
K	36	K	35	F	163
L	29	J	21	C	141
J	14	F	16	G	110
D⎫	7	G	9	A	109
G⎭	7	L	8	D	102
F	3	D	7	J	63
I	2	I	3	I	3

Source: Compiled by the authors.

A method of discriminating between these hypotheses is to calculate the zero-order correlation coefficients between cost-effectiveness and cost and effectiveness respectively; these correlations are shown below:

	Zero Order Correlation Coefficients	
	---	---
	Cost	Effectiveness
Cost Effectiveness	-.4	.4

These correlation coefficients have the expected signs, but are insignificant. A further hypothesis is that cost-effectiveness is a function of both costs and effectiveness together, that is, $CE = f(C,E)$. But the zero-order multiple correlation coefficient between cost-effectiveness and cost and effectiveness is 0.4, which is again insignificant. It may be concluded, therefore, that the cost-effectiveness of a particular service is a function of many factors.

The evidence on what these influences may be is rather limited, but in the first instance it seems to be connected to some extent with the type of service produced. Of the 12 services considered, 9 were basically abstracting services. The exceptions are D, which is enquiry answering, and G and L, which are SDI services. The enquiry-answering service does not reach more than ninth place in any of the cost-effectiveness rankings, while the SDI services reach fourth place in the Dependence Index ranking and only seventh and ninth places in the C_1 and E_1 rankings respectively. This would suggest that the method of disseminating information in the form of abstracting services is comparatively economic.

It should be possible to improve greatly on the cost-effectiveness results for individual services by using the subscription lists of the services as a sample frame. Where the subscriber is a firm, the users could be sampled in the same way as in this study, and the estimation procedures would be largely similar to those used here. The cost-effectiveness values obtained for each service in this way would be more statistically significant

OTHER RESULTS

It is possible both to compare the similarity between different measures and to throw light on the information situation within industry in general. The major comparisons concern the C and E values and their relation to the estimates of value given by the information officiers and budget allocators in the firms.

Comparisons between the C_1 and E_1 measures yielded an r^2 of 0.63 with coefficients significant at the 5 percent level. The addition into the regression of the number of R & D workers in the firms improved the fit with a resulting r^2 of 0.81. The improvement here is a reflection of the multiplication of differences between C_1 and E_1 in the aggregation process in the firms with large numbers of R & D personnel. The comparison between C_2 and E_2 shows a closer relation, as might be expected since less is being added to the A measure in each case. Here an r^2 of 0.81 was found with an improvement in explanation to an r^2 of 0.88. The C measure is found to vary in proportion to E with a coefficient of between 0.5 and 0.7 in the instances above, with the coefficients being significant at the 5 percent level.

The Wessel and Moore report relies heavily on the views of information officers.[1] It was the experience of the present study that as far as individual secondary information services were concerned there was little feedback between information officers and users. Therefore, it was felt unwise to rely on the information officer's estimate and consequently alternative methods were devised. The moment has now come to examine the relation between the estimates derived from the information officers and the individual users in the case of specific services.

The results found from regressing the C and E values against the information officer's values derived from the answers to questions 4(b) and 4(c) of Part one of the questionnaire showed no significant relationship, tentatively justifying the procedures used in this study. It was thought that the inclusion of either, or both, the number of

R & D workers or the total information budget might yield an explanation of this, but this was not so, with no significant result being obtained.

The comparison between the information officer's estimate and the budget allocator's estimate yielded an r^2 of 0.998. This suggests that the budget allocator relies entirely on the information officer's judgment in making his decision. With 20 observations here, the coefficient in the regression is 1.001 with significance at better than the 1 percent level.

We must now ask what conclusions can be drawn from the lack of any relationship between our measures and those of the information officers. There are several possible interpretations:

1. The information officer's estimate may include an estimate of the value of the information to departments other than the R & D department.

2. The information officer's estimate may include a value for external information as in input, not to the formal information service they provide, for this is already included, but to any informal information network. There is no way of the individual research worker estimating such a value.

3. The information officer may value each item partly because it is useful to him in drawing up internally circulated secondary information bulletins, that is, in providing a technical information service. R & D workers may not be aware of the importance of individual sources for this service.

4. Our procedures may be faulty, either through the weighting given to different information users, through sampling error, or through defective questionnaire procedure.

5. The information officer's subjective estimates may be faulty.

It would require further study to determine which of these interpretations provides the best explanation of the observed result.

It was interesting to contrast three other items of data with the number of R & D workers. First, the cost of technical information services was regressed against the number of R & D workers and was found to yield an r^2 of 0.56 with a coefficient of 1.86 significant at the 5 percent level. There were 80 observations here and no account was taken of those firms that do not provide an internal service.

Similarly, the firms' information budget, when regressed on the number of R & D workers, produced an r^2 of 0.41 and a coefficient of 1.06 significant at the 5 percent level.

Finally, the number of information staff employed by the firms was found to bear no relation to the number of R & D workers in the firms.

It might be valuable to attempt some measurement of the "optima" expenditure on technical information services within the firms. It should be stressed here that the greatest value in the following exercise may lie simply in demonstrating the various methods by which this measure could be achieved. However, where independent methods suggest expenditure of the same order of magnitude, it may be possible to regard the results as rewarding in themselves.

Throughout the discussion, information expenditure per R & D worker is examined rather than the less relevant and less useful information expenditure per firm.

Method 1. Average System

The first and most simple approach that suggests itself is examination of the average expenditure per R & D worker observed in this survey (See Table 4.23).

It might be considered that most firms that lag behind in this relatively new field of information would derive greater benefit by moving to the average information expenditure per R & D worker. Sampling techniques unfortunately prohibit an analysis that would allow for different disciplines and subject fields and their diverse information needs and reasonably accurate analysis can only be made for industry breakdowns.

Method 2. Information-Conscious System

A slightly less crude system, although not unlike Method 1, would be to examine the expenditure per R & D worker of those firms that are labeled information-conscious (Table 4.24). One suggestion would be that all firms in the respective industries might benefit from following the example of firms widely familiar with both research and development and information systems.

TABLE 4.23

All Firms: Information Expenditure per R & D Worker
(in pounds)

Industry	Information Expenditure
Agriculture	114
Aircraft	38
Chemical	276
Electrical engineering	177
Textiles	165
All Industries	133

Source: Compiled by the authors.

TABLE 4.24

Information-Conscious Firms:
Information Expenditure per R & D Worker
(in pounds)

Industry	Information Expenditure
Agriculture	96
Aircraft	18
Chemical	275
Electrical engineering	256
Textile	164
All Industries	170

Source: Compiled by the authors.

This system suggests that, on average, more should be spent on information, especially in the electrical engineering industry.

Method 3. Reasonable Budget System

The third method of obtaining some measure of the most suitable information expenditure per R & D worker derives from Part Two of the questionnaire.* Here the budget allocator is asked for his estimate of a reasonable sum to be allocated for information purposes. From this data it is possible to draw up a chart for each industry (Table 4.25).

As Table 4.25 demonstrates, the estimated reasonable information budget per R & D worker is on the whole (with the most obvious exception of electrical engineering) higher than the current average expenditure for information-conscious and other firms. The marked deviations over industries are not inconsistent with the deviations present in the current average information expenditure of the different industries.

Method 4. Constant Rate of Surplus System

The hypotheses to be tested for this method concern the relationship between the surplus earned by information activity, the size of information expenditure, and the number of R & D workers. If it can be shown that the surplus earned by information expenditure is in

---

*See Appendix A.

TABLE 4.25

Reasonable Information Expenditure per R & D Worker
(in pounds)

Industry	Over All Firms	Information-Conscious Firms	Other
Agriculture	103	80	121
Aircraft	146	–	146
Chemical	535	399	554
Electrical engineering	108	258	92
Textiles	173	201	162
Total	254	210	263

Source: Compiled by the authors.

some part explained by one or both of the other two variables, then this relationship can be used to suggest policy for future information expenditure. "Surplus" may be defined as the difference between the value or utility derived from any given amount of a commodity and its total cost.² A simple estimate of the surplus can be obtained in the case of secondary information for each firm by subtracting the expenditure on information from a monetary measure of value to give V - X (where V = value in £, and X = £ expenditure on information). Two measures of value or utility (V) are used, $C_1 = A + B$ and $C_2 = A + \frac{1}{2}B$. In view of the high correlation between C and E values it was felt unnecessary to use the latter as alternative measures in the following regressions. A measure of the rate of surplus is obtained by dividing the estimate of the surplus, V - X, by the expenditure to give V - X/X. The first two regressions were conducted to test the hypothesis that the rate of surplus is dependent upon expenditure.* It might be expected, for example, that as expenditure rises the rate of surplus decreases. The results show such a hypothesis to be unsupported: the coefficient of X, although negative, is not significant.

$$\pi_1 = 5.5 - 0.00002X \quad R^2 = .0033 \quad (1)$$
$$\quad\quad (.97)\ (.00005)$$

$$\pi_2 = 4.5 - 0.00003X \quad R^2 = .0075 \quad (2)$$
$$\quad\quad (.82)\ (.00004)$$

---

*$\pi_1 = \dfrac{C_1 - X}{X}$ and $\pi_2 = \dfrac{C_2 - X}{X}$

The R^2's yield the conclusion that changes in expenditure explain less than 1 percent of the variations in the rate of surplus. The correlation coefficient between π_1 and X is -0.058 and between π_2 and X_1 -0.087.

The second hypothesis tested was that the rate of surplus, π, is dependent upon the number of R & D staff, as well as on expenditure. Here the regressions are found to be significant with coefficients significant at the 5 percent level, although the R^2's are not high, 0.34 and 0.28 respectively.

$$\pi_1 = 3.9 - 0.00017X + .043S \quad R^2 = 0.34 \quad (3)$$
$$(8.5) \quad (.00005) \quad (.008)$$

$$\pi_2 = 3.2 - 0.00014X + 0.033S \quad R^2 = 0.28 \quad (4)$$
$$(.75) \quad (.00004) \quad (.007)$$

Although this hypothesis only explains just over one-third of the variations in the surplus, it is possible to say that the rate of surplus gained through information expenditure rises with increases in R & D staff and declined slowly with increases in expenditure. It is also possible, using equation 3, which gives the best fit, to make some tentative suggestions concerning information expenditure policy.

$$\pi_1 = 3.9 - 0.00017X + .043S \quad (3)$$

In order to maintain a constant rate of surplus

$$\frac{d\pi_1}{dX} = 0$$

$$\frac{d\pi_1}{dX} = -0.0017 = 0.043 \frac{dS}{dX}$$

for constant

$$\frac{dS}{dX} = \frac{0.00017}{0.043} = 0.00395 \quad (5)$$

From some points of view it might be thought that firms should aim at maximizing their total surplus, although on the assumption that the present average rate of surplus is reasonably appropriate, firms would benefit from maintaining constancy. The latter approach suggests using the information in equation 5: that for firms to maintain a constant rate of surplus on their information expenditure, for every extra R & D worker employed a sum of £253 should be allocated for information purposes.

There are many qualifications that must be made at this point; the R^2 is not high; the estimates of utility may well be biased upward,

TABLE 4.26

Estimates of Suitable Expenditure per R & D Worker

Industry	Method 1	Method 2	Method 3	Method 4
Agriculture	114	96	103	—
Aircraft	38	18	146	—
Chemical	276	275	535	—
Electrical engineering	177	256	108	—
Textile	165	164	173	—
Total	133	170	254	253

Source: Compiled by the authors.

giving an upward bias to the evaluation of the surplus. Above all it should be mentioned that the regression analysis has been conducted over firms and industries that have a wide range of information needs and that enjoy varying degrees of benefit from using secondary information. It may therefore seem presumptuous to suggest any kind of optimum behavior that could apply to all interests alike. However, the figure of £253 tallies remarkably with the overall figure of £254 obtained by Method 3 and with the expenditure of the majority of information-conscious firms in Method 2.

Table 4.26 shows that the average system, Method 1, yields, on the whole, lower estimates than the other methods, although even adherence to this method would involve considerable marking up of expenditure for several firms. The other three methods yield rather similar results, mostly suggesting raises in expenditure from the current level.

SUMMARY AND CONCLUSIONS

1. It appears practicable to develop a technique for evaluating the relative effectiveness of alternative secondary information systems. The relative effectiveness of these different systems depends largely on the number of R & D workers served.

2. Such techniques depend essentially upon a survey of the opinions of R & D staff utilizing the information services. The estimates made by information officers differ markedly from these valuations.

3. Pure abstracting services appear to offer substantially greater benefit to users than alternative secondary information systems.

4. Detailed information may be obtained through the techniques developed on the different information needs of users of different background and employment. This material is potentially of value in forecasting secondary information requirements.

5. A technique is suggested for investigating the reasons for the different valuations given to the different secondary information services by evaluating the characteristics of the services.

6. The cost of abstracting services appears to depend largely on the length of the abstract produced.

7. There are no apparent economies of scale in the production of abstracts. On the other hand, economies from amalgamation of secondary information systems appear to be available but this can best be resolved by detailed investigation.

8. Cost-effectiveness measures are shown to depend only partly on relative effectiveness or relative costs. There seems no alternative to a detailed investigation of both costs and effectiveness if reliable estimates are to be made.

9. Some tentative suggestions based on several different methods of calculation, are made concerning the "optimal" level of expenditure on internal technical information systems per R & D worker.

NOTES

1. C. S. Wessel and K. L. Moore, Criteria for Evaluating the Effectiveness of Library Operations and Services Army Technical Library Improvement Studies, Report no. 21 (Washington, D.C., January 1969).

2. J. Robinson, Economics of Imperfect Competition, (London: Macmillan, 1933).

CHAPTER

5

CONCLUSIONS

This chapter is designed to provide an overall survey of our work; to state and praise the intention and to lament the many places where, in this early state of the art, we have not yet been able to achieve our objectives or have faltered on the way.

First of all then, the intention: we have sought to apply an economic calculus to a range of problems—economic choice without price constraint—not usually treated by economists. We have noted the wide range of phenomena involved. We have noted too the virtual necessity of relying to some extent upon the reports rather than actions of the individuals we are studying. If we were to succeed we might open a route that could help reduce drastically the range of policy options open to firms and government. Of course difficulties would still remain, and particularly difficulties over the distribution of services among the different claimants and the extent to which different distributions involve different volumes of production of different commodities or services, with consequent variation in technology, cost, factor incomes, and total production.

The actuality falls far short of such a goal. It falls short for a number of reasons. The most obvious is that the total exercise was far too small, and the number of secondary information suppliers far too few to obtain a satisfactory range of cost-effectiveness estimates.

Even at the level of effectiveness measures, however, there are many shortcomings. One of our measures depends upon the subjective estimates of certain objective facts, the effect of less information work upon research output. It is not really satisfactory to answer that such a relationship is linear and proportional. This may not be true even at the micro level, and the effects of aggregation are at best unpredictable. Furthermore, there is little reason to feel assured of any definite relationship between the subjective assignment of value to a service and the valuation as observed from actual choices, even if we manage to phrase our questions so as to eliminate any possible advantage in lying.

The problem is partly one of comparing subjective preferences of this sort against choice behavior in experimental situations to see what relationships, if any, can be seen to arise. Partly, however, this problem arises because of the different techniques used for ascertaining choices at different points, and thus the amalgamation of these measures in our study. More strikingly, however, difficulty may arise because of the varying interpretations by respondents of some of the questions.

Thus there may be differences in the meanings attached by individuals surveyed to such apparently obvious instructions as "Divide 100 points between X and Y (two alternative bodies of services)." The economist might readily point out the ambiguity: is the division to be proportional to consumers' surplus of the two services, or proportional to the marginal rate of substitution? Or is it to be some amalgamation of the two? We have no direct evidence of the proportion of those questioned who will adopt one or another of the possible interpretations. There is important psychoeconomic work to be done on this question before the conception employed in this work can be more widely used with some confidence. How, for example, does the interpretation of the respondent vary with his age, his education, his exposure to economic training, and so on? Again we must ask the extent to which our questions are interpreted in a partial equilibrium sense, with the supply of all other services held constant, and the extent to which mental adjustment is made for the availability of substitutes. It has seemed reasonable in a fairly large sample, and for a first attempt, to disregard these problems, assuming that whatever distribution of interpretations existed between respondents would arise in each subgroup studied. Such an assumption may possibly pass muster the first time around, but it obviously calls for deeper study in the future.

One point worthy of careful thought in future studies is our procedure of utilizing individual, presumably subjective, estimates of the objective influence of secondary information on work patterns and research output. The alternative procedure of finding physical and objective benefits, made familiar in traffic studies, is obviously more satisfactory if it is available. In a large class of cases such objective measures are not readily available, however, and other alternatives must be investigated. Information appeared to be one such difficult case. It is possible that the subjective element could be diminished to some degree in further studies. It should be made crystal clear that a reduction in the subjective component of cost-effectiveness studies is desirable wherever possible.

The approaches considered have been devoted to the examination of the costs and benefits of existing services. The costs have been national in scope and the benefits have also been national. There are several ways in which it would be possible to extend this analysis. We might extend the constituency covered so as to deal with the international aspects. The problem might be redefined so that the focus of attention is on the national costs and benefits of participating in a particular international scheme of cooperation. The analysis might be switched from the consideration of total existing schemes to the appraisal of potential new schemes—that is, reformulated in terms of an investment appraisal format. And finally we may utilize our present viewpoint to consider the advantages of providing some existing service in a new (for example, more capital-intensive) form.

There has been a growing tendency to think in terms of international cooperation in the field of secondary information services. This arises partly because some of the computer-based systems of information storage and retrieval are only economical if conducted on a larger scale than can be made possible in any single country. Sometimes it arises, too, because a particular large information user sees such proposals as a means of obtaining further financial support for a scheme already decided on with only the national market in mind. One possible line of thought is that the world as a whole ought to be considered as the proper constituency for any cost-benefit analysis of information systems. Schemes might be desirable in terms of such a constituency that would not be advantageous when viewed from the standpoint of any one country.

It would be wrong to ignore the many policy issues that lie concealed behind any such analysis. In the first place there is the difficulty of giving a proper weighting to costs arising in different countries; an hour's work or a dollar of resources may have an entirely different significance in different countries. Second, there is the problem of weighting the benefits accruing to different countries; a dollar's worth of benefit may have an entirely different significance in a poor country from what it has in a rich one. And finally there is the point that the economic competition among countries is a real phenomenon, as real as feelings of international solidarity. A position of technological leadership confers benefits in terms of standards of living to the workers in a country that possesses it. And therefore a technological gain on the part of one country may well be realized at the expense of the technological leadership and hence the standard of living of another. It is perhaps true that in the long run all must gain by technological progress, but the distribution of the gains is very much at issue at any moment, and some stand to lose in the short run. A similar difficulty arises in the more limited national study upon which we have focused attention in this volume: consider our practice of adding the benefits to competing firms to obtain a national total benefit, thus ignoring interfirm competition and competition between the different regions of a country.

Another manageable problem is the consideration of the national advantage with respect to participation in a particular international scheme. Here the advantage to be considered is national in scope. Correspondingly, the costs in this context are those borne by national residents or national firms. (Some adjustment ought perhaps strictly to be made for dividends paid to shareholders resident abroad.) The difference between costs and benefits represents the maximum value that will accrue to any given country as a result of participation in the scheme. The actual value of participation may be less than this if a nationally based substitute arrangement is possible. Consider, for example, a particular international scheme I with national benefits B_I and national costs C_I. The net national benefit from participation cannot exceed N_I where:

$$N_I = B_I - C_I \tag{1}$$

Suppose now that there is some national scheme with national costs C_S and national benefits B_S (all calculated on the assumption that no costs or benefits of the international scheme are suffered or enjoyed). Then the net national benefit of scheme S, which we will call N_S is given by:

$$N_S \lessgtr B_S - C_S \tag{2}$$

Now the true gain from entering the international scheme V_I must be equal to or less than the net gain from the international scheme minus the net gain from undertaking the national scheme, that is,

$$V_I \lessgtr N_I - N_S \lessgtr (B_I - B_S) - (C_I - C_S) \tag{3}$$

and this value V_I indicates the maximum net value from joining the international scheme.

We now consider the value to the individual firm of any particular element of its secondary information system. The points to be noted in this case include the fact that the costs that must be considered are only those that are borne by the individual firm, and similarly for the benefits enjoyed. Care must be taken too in considering the extent to which the benefits accruing to the firm are identical with those used in calculating national benefits; in general, firms may be expected to gain something from competitive advantage over their rivals and while we may assume that any such competitive gain can be equalized by a change in net resources devoted to research and development, the existence of expenditure constraints involves a complicating factor. Again attention must be paid to the fact that each element of the secondary information system is evaluated on the assumption that its withdrawal would not affect the availability of other elements in the secondary information system. Since all the elements in the secondary information system are connected by complex relationships of substitution and complementarity, there is a limit to the reliance that can be placed on measures of the total worth of the secondary information system available to the firm by summing the separate values attached to each of its component parts.

Care must be taken to give proper weight to the specific shortages and anxieties that confront the particular firm. These perhaps may be ignored as a first approximation when dealing with national benefits, but in the particular firm, special attention will have to be paid to these factors, which may include such things as labor turnover, the shortage of scientists of a particular grade or discipline, or unusual restrictions on the information budget. These specific problems may in general be handled by the use of shadow prices for factors of production in a way familiar to economists and students of operations research literature.

It is a characteristic of the approach adopted in this volume that attention is focused on the cost and value of specific secondary information inputs taken as a unit rather than considered from an incremental point of view. Moreover, our approach has focused on existing services rather than on new services whose introduction is proposed. Our approach is made more plausible if we assume that there will be no change in demand or in cost in the future. It is possible to develop a rationalization for this procedure, and yet it limits the immediate applicability of our results to investment appraisal.

The utilization for investment appraisal of the estimates produced by our method depends on the assumption that increments of expenditure on services yielding high bonuses of benefits over costs will prove to be advantageous. Put more technically, this comes to the assumption that the incremental value of expenditure on some particular service, K, is related to the surplus produced by the existing volume of the service T. Hence if $Z_K(T)$ is the surplus and $C_K(T)$ and $B_K(T)$ are the costs and benefits associated with the service at its present intensity T, then:

$$Z_K(T) = B_K(T) - C_K(T)$$

and our proposition is that:

$$\frac{d}{dT}\left[Z_K(T)\right] = F\left[\frac{Z_K(T)}{T}\right]$$

where F is an increasing positive function and T may be expressed in terms of costs. Assuming proportionality, we may write this expression as:

$$\frac{d}{dC_K}\left[Z_K(T)\right] = A\left[\frac{Z_K(T)}{C_K(T)}\right] = A\left[\frac{B_K(T)}{C_K(T)} - 1\right]$$

where A is a positive constant of proportionality. Put in this way it will be seen that our procedure implies certain restrictions on the form of the surplus function that are not altogether uncontroversial.

There is an important element of ambiguity concealed behind the apparent accuracy of this mathematical formula. It stems from the fact that greater intensity of application of a particular form of secondary information activity is likely to involve a distinct change in the character of the service provided. Thus our formulation might be most attractive when dealing with, let us say, the expenditure of more money to obtain more exact or more revealing abstracts. If, on the other hand, the increase in expenditure involved the introduction of an indexing service in addition to a given abstracting service, a change of form would be involved and difficulties would be bound to arise.

It would seem possible to extend this basic assumption about the relationship between estimates of surplus and of incremental benefit to a model in which the utilization of a given service was growing (perhaps because of an underlying increase in the research personnel in the industries most concerned) or in which costs were declining (perhaps because of increased familiarity with the particular information problems involved). In such cases it would be necessary to make estimates of the rates of movement of the key variables affecting benefit and cost. And some system of appropriately discounting all future costs and benefits to the present would be necessary.

A more complete form of investment appraisal is conceptually possible, involving the assessment of the net value of the introduction of some presently unavailable service. Such an appraisal, besides requiring estimates of the future developments of costs and demand and the introduction of an appropriate discounting factor, would require an appraisal of the costs and benefits of the new service. The most difficult problem is the estimation of the value of benefits from the new service. Two alternative methods are available. The first would be experimental and would require the introduction of the new techniques on a pilot basis with limited coverage and for a limited time. Such an experimental approach is, however, likely to prove expensive at best and inconclusive at worst. The second method would depend upon the evaluation of the new service in terms of its component characteristics. Each of those characteristics could be evaluated for the particular constituency involved and a benefit balance struck.

Sometimes a proposed change involves little or no alteration in the form of service and hence little or no alteration in the benefit situation. In such a case the sole change may be in the cost dimension and the investment appraisal problem will be very greatly simplified. For a full appraisal it still will be necessary to estimate the growth of usage, the trend of costs, and the discount factor.

In any investment appraisal it will be necessary to estimate whether and to what extent reduced costs will be passed on in the form of reduced prices for the service involved and the extent to which these hypothetical reduced prices will alter the number of those who are enabled to make use of the information service concerned. In short, it will be necessary to estimate the sensitivity of prices to costs, and the elasticity of demand for the service with consequent effects on prices and demand. This is a complex task, and one that has not been attempted in the present volume. But it appears to be within the scope of existing econometric techniques.

APPENDIX A

THE QUESTIONNAIRE

UNIVERSITY OF EDINBURGH   CONFIDENTIAL
Department of Economics

Assessment of the benefits of information systems

PART ONE: INFORMATION OFFICER OR LIBRARIAN

Introduction

The aim of the enquiry is to estimate the relative value of different types of information services, with the ultimate object of making suggestions for improving these services. The types of information services in which we are interested are those providing secondary information, i.e. references to original papers, reports, patents, etc., rather than the primary information contained in these documents. Examples of secondary information are abstracts, titles lists, etc.

The information you give will not be disclosed to anyone but will be combined with other similar information to obtain a general view.

Name of establishment

Interviewer   date

1. Would you please tell me how many persons are engaged in research and development within the establishment?

    How many staff including clerical staff are employed in the information/library services?

    (a) full-time
    (b) part-time   express in full-time equivalent

    And how many of these are clerical?

(a) full-time
(b) part-time express in full-time equivalent

2. Please list the information services that the establishment takes including free ones and those the establishment provides itself, under the headings given on the check sheet.

   Are any of the external services obtained in more than one copy, or by more than one subscription? Please name.

   Please list the total cost of subscriptions per year for each external service.

3. Of the abstract journals used by the establishment are any outstandingly important?

4. (a) If you provide an internal information service of the type listed on the check sheet, please state the approximate total cost of the service per annum.
   £

   (b) In order to indicate the relative values of the inputs to the internal service, please distribute 100 points between internal and external inputs.
   External
   Internal

   (c) In order to indicate the relative value of the individual external information services that are used as inputs to the internal service, please distribute 100 points between these services. Insert answer in check list.

5. If there were no financial constraints on your budget, and in view of the amount of use of information that is made at present within the establishment, what in your own mind would be a reasonable additional amount to spend, in the following circumstances.

   (a) On external secondary information services, given no increase in staff?
   %

   (b) On staff, given no increase in external secondary information services?
   %

(c) On both staff and external services, if the two could be increased?

%

6. If you chose to spend more on external information services, which services would you purchase?

7. If your expenditure on secondary information services were cut by 50 percent, how would the cut be distributed among the different categories of service given on the check sheet? Please name which services in each category would no longer be purchased.

8. If the price of each service that you take at present were to increase by 50 percent you would presumably cut back on the number of services that you purchase. How would you distribute the cut among the different categories of service given on the check sheet? Please name which services in each category would no longer be purchased?

9. (a) What would the cost to the establishment be if it had to provide all the secondary information used within the establishment from each of the following external services?

   (b) If the annual purchase prices for each of the services named in question 9(a) were to rise, at what level would the establishment stop subscribing to these services?

   Q.9(a)   Q.9(b)

   (i) Abstracts
   (ii) Titles lists
   (iii) SDI services
   (iv) Enquiry-answering services
   (v) Other

10. What price would you be prepared to pay for the secondary publications you obtain from research associations or learned societies if they were not included in the subscriptions but priced separately?

11. (a) Which other secondary information services that you are aware of cover the fields you serve at present?

    (b) Would a change in price induce you to purchase any of these?

If so, at what price would you purchase each of the services? Please indicate the present price of these services. Insert answers on check list 2.

Thank you for your help. Have you any particular comments you think might be of help to us?

CHECK LIST FOR ESTABLISHMENTS 1

Name of service	Number of copies	Cost	Relative value of input to internal service
Abstracts (i) Pure abstracts			
(ii) Abstracts in primary journals			
(iii) Abstracts in research association bulletins			
Titles lists			
Enquiry-answering services			
Selective dissemination of information services (SDI)			
Others			

CHECK LIST FOR ESTABLISHMENTS 2

Name of service	Q.7	Q.8	Q.10	Q.11

Abstracts
(i)   Pure abstracts

(ii) Abstracts in primary journals

(iii) Abstracts in research
      association bulletins

Titles lists

Enquiry-answering services

Selective disseminations
of information services (SDI)

Others

CHECK SHEET

Categories of Secondary Information Service

1. Abstracts

    (i)   Pure abstracts
    (ii) Primary journals containing a section with abstracts
    (iii) Research association bulletins containing a section with abstracts

2. Titles lists

3. Enquiry-answering services

4. SDI (Selective dissemination of information) services

5. Others

PART TWO: RESEARCH DIRECTOR OR BUDGET ALLOCATOR

Introduction

The aim of the enquiry is to estimate the relative value of different types of information services, with the ultimate object of making suggestions for improving these services. The types of information services in which we are interested are those providing secondary information, that is, references to original papers, reports, patents, etc., rather than the primary information contained in these documents. Examples of secondary information are abstracts, titles lists, etc.

The information you give will not be disclosed to any one but will be combined with other similar information to obtain a general view.

Name of establishment

Interviewer   date

1. (a) Please give an indication of the size of your present annual information budget.
   £

   (b) Do you decide the total expenditure of the information department?

   (c) Assuming no particular financial pressures, what would you regard as being a reasonable total sum to spend on secondary information services in the light of the research and development going on at present in the establishment and the current use being made of secondary information services?
   £

2. If your expenditure on secondary information services were cut by 50 percent, how would the cut be distributed among the different categories of service given on the check list? Please name which services in each category would no longer be purchased.

3. If the price of each service that you take at present were to increase by 50 percent, you would presumably cut back on the number of services that you purchase. How would you distribute the cut among the different categories of service given on the

check sheet?* Please name which services in each category would no longer be purchased.

4. (a) What would the cost to the establishment be if it had to provide all the secondary information used within the establishment from each of the following external services?

   (b) If the annual purchase prices for each of the services named in question 4(a) were to rise, at what price level would the establishment stop subscribing to these services?

                                                    Q.4(a)   Q.4(b)

      (i) Abstracts
     (ii) Titles lists
    (iii) SDI services
    (iv) Enquiry-answering services
     (v) Other

5. What price would you be prepared to pay for the secondary journals you obtain from reserach associations or learned societies if they were produced independently of the organizations and therefore not included in its subscriptions?

Thank you for your help. Have you any particular comments you think might be of help to us?

---

*See p. 119.

CHECK LIST FOR BUDGET ALLOCATOR

Category of service	Question 2	Question 3
Abstracts (i) Pure abstracts		
(ii) Abstracts in primary journals		
(iii) Abstracts in research association bulletins		
Titles lists		
Enquiry-answering services		
Selective dissemination of information services (SDI)		
Others		

PART THREE: INDIVIDUAL MEMBER OF STAFF

Introduction

The aim of the enquiry is to estimate the relative value of different types of information services, with the ultimate object of making suggestions for improving these services. The types of information services in which we are interested are those providing secondary information, that is, references to original papers, reports, patents, etc., rather than the primary information contained in these documents. Examples of secondary information are abstracts, titles lists, etc.

The information you give will not be disclosed to anyone but will be combined with other similar information to obtain a general view.

Name of establishment

Interviewer   date

1. (a) Would you describe yourself as being engaged in pure science or applied science?

    If applied science, which of the following types of work do you undertake?

    (i) Research
    (ii) Development
    (iii) Other, specify

   (b) What proportion of your working week is spent on

    (i) Research and development and related information work
    (ii) Other activities

   (c) Please indicate field of interest, that is, discipline and subject field within discipline.

2. How many years have you been employed in applied research and development work, whether for your present employers or others?

3. (a) Which of the following types of information do you seek in the course of your work?

    (i) Information for keeping up to date in a general and continuous way (current awareness).

(ii) Information for a specific research or development project or problem (information retrieval)
(iii) Other, specify

For the remainder of the questionnaire, we will refer to current awareness and information retrieval as defined above.

(b) What proportion of your information needs that are met by secondary information is represented by the need for

(i) Current awareness?
(ii) Information retrieval?
(iii) Other?

4. (a) Which information services, both internal and external, do you use?

(b) For what purpose do you use these services?

(c) Do you pay, partially or wholly, for any of them? If yes, which ones and how much?

5. (a) Of the total time you spend on research and development, what proportion of this time is spent seeking information and reading published information?

(b) And what proportion of the time spent seeking information and reading published information is spent on using secondary information services?

6. Please distribute about 100 points among the following four sources of secondary information in order to give an indication of their relative value to you in your research and development work.

1. All secondary information services that you use
2. Trade literature
3. Personal contact within the establishment
4. Personal contact outside the establishment

7. Which services do you make most use of?

(i)
(ii)
(iii)
(iv)

8. If your present sources of secondary information disappeared, which alternative sources would you use to satisfy your information needs?

Type of Information Need

Current	Retrieval	Other

9. In choosing a particular information service to meet your needs for information, your choice will tend to be influenced by certain characteristics possessed by the information service. Examples of such characteristics are given on the check sheet. There may be others you can think of.

   (a) For each of your information needs, that is, current, retrieval, or other, please indicate the characteristics you deem to be important in relation to that need. To these, please assign a mark on a scale from 1-10 to indicate degree of importance. A mark of 10 would imply that a given characteristic was essential.

   (b) Let us assume that you are given the opportunity of bringing about a small improvement in the group of information services you use to meet a particular information need, that is, current, retrieval, or other. For each information need please indicate to which characteristic or characteristics you would apply the improvement, in order of importance.

Characteristic	Type of information need					
	Current		Retrieval		Other	
	Q.9(a)	Q.9(b)	Q.9(a)	Q.9(b)	Q.9(a)	Q.9(b)
Speed in publication of secondary information or speed in reply to enquiry						
Coverage of field of interest						
Relevance to your need						
Degree of detail in content of information supplied						
Subject arrangement or classification						
Indexing						
Supply of additional services from the same location						

Others

10. For each of your information needs, that is, current, retrieval, or other, please indicate on a scale from 0-100 how satisfied you are in respect to each characteristic with the services of which you make most use.

Characteristic	Service	Type of information need		
		Current	Retrieval	Other
Speed in publication of secondary information or speed in reply to enquiry	i ii iii iv			
Coverage of field of interest	i ii iii iv			
Relevance to your need	i ii iii iv			
Degree of detail in content of information supplied	i ii iii iv			
Subject arrangement or classification	i ii iii iv			
Indexing	i ii iii iv			
Supply of additional services from the same location	i ii iii iv			
Others	i ii iii iv			

11. (a) Please indicate the value of all the secondary information work undertaken on your behalf within the firm, on a scale from 0-50. 50 represents the value of the situation in which all of the information you require, but no more, is available to you exactly as you require it.

   (b) In order to indicate the relative value to you of all secondary information services that you use, please distribute about 100 points amongst them, with high scores representing high values. Insert answers on check list.

The following three questions refer to hypothetical situations and are aimed at finding an indication of the value you put on the secondary information services you use.

12. Compare the present situation in which you and your colleagues have access to all the secondary information services with the hypothetical one in which none of these is available to any of you.

   If you had the choice of having your present job with secondary information services at your present salary, or the same job with no secondary information services and an increased salary, how much increase in salary would you require before choosing the situation where no secondary information services were available?

0	£200-£ 300
£ 0-£ 10	300- 400
10- 20	400- 500
20- 30	500- 600
30- 40	600- 700
40- 50	700- 800
50- 100	800- 900
100- 200	900- 1,000

   If greater than £1,000, Then £

13. (a) In the same hypothetical situation, with none of the services available to you, you may choose to spend some extra time in doing your own information work, or you may choose to adjust to the situation in some other way.

In order to show what you would do, please indicate the changes you would make in the number of hours you would devote to:

    (i) Research and development work, not including information work
    (ii) Information work
    (iii) Other work

(b) If you reduce your research time, this will presumably reduce your research output. How many extra hours would you have to maintain your previous research output?

(c) Please indicate the weekly average number of hours that you work.

14. Please indicate on a scale from 0-50 how important secondary information services are to you in your research and development work. 50 represents a situation of total dependence.

15. It would be very helpful if you would give the following information. This information will be treated in fullest confidence.

    (a) Year of birth
    (b) Current annual rate of salary

Thank you for your help. Have you any particular comments you think might be of help to us?

CHECK LIST

Name of service	Current	Retrieval	Other	Payment	Value
Abstracts (i) Pure abstracts					
(ii) Abstracts in primary journals					
(iii) Abstracts in research association bulletins					
Titles lists					
Enquiry-answering services					
Selective Dissemination of Information Services (SDI)					
Others					

CHECK SHEET

Questions 8 & 9

Characteristic	Type of information need		
	Current	Retrieval	Other
Speed in publication of secondary information (or speed in reply to enquiry)			
Coverage of field of interest			
Relevance to your need			
Degree of detail in content of information supplied			
Subject arrangement or classification			
Indexing			
Supply of additional services from the same location			
Others			

APPENDIX B

SAMPLE FRAME

The description of the process of sampling is to be found in the appropriate place; the purpose of this appendix is simply to give a detailed note of where the present sample was found.

The sample was drawn from "Guide to Key British Enterprise," 5th ed. (London: Dun & Bradstreet Ltd., 1969). The industries were selected as follows:

Agriculture	S.I.C.*	001.1, 001.2, 001.3.
Chemical	S.I.C	271.1, 271.2, 271.3
		272.1, 272.2
		273
		274
		275.2
		277.2
Electrical	S.I.C.	339.3
		341.2, 341.3
		351.4
		361
		362
		363
		364.1, 364.2, 364.3
		365
		369.1, 369.2, 369.3, 369.4, 369.5.
Aircraft	S.I.C.	383
		384.2
		385.2
Textile	S.I.C.	411
		412
		413.2
		414.1, 414.2, 414.3, 414.5, 414.6,
		415
		416
		417
		418
		419
		421
		422
		423
		429

*S.I.C. Standard Industrial Classification.

APPENDIX C

COST MANUAL

Introduction

This manual provides a standardized procedure for collecting the costs of systems that produce and disseminate secondary information, with the objectives of calculating cost-effectiveness ratios and indicators.

The production components in the field of secondary information are not always uniquely definable, and it is therefore not possible to establish a specific step-by-step procedure that will serve in all cases. A certain amount of discretion must be assumed by the individual performing the costing exercise, and one of the purposes of this manual is to establish where this discretion is likely to arise and how it should be exercised.

The manual also provides a background to the field of information and should, in itself, provide the basis for a familiarization course to enable persons other than those who have previously specialized in information work to perform costing studies. It also serves to specify those aspects of information work in which we are interested as well as going some way toward establishing a common nomenclature.

This is a practical manual but discussions are entered into at times to aid in the process of familiarization as well as serving as a practical help to the individual performing the costing; however, no excursions are made into the realms of economic theory that underly many of the steps in the method.

The Production of Secondary Information

In the first instance it is necessary to establish a basis on which to identify the production unit that is to be costed, and this production unit will henceforth be referred to as an information system.

The first step here is to examine the various outputs of information systems that are normally classified as secondary information, and then the information system itself may be discussed and identified in light of this.

Secondary Information

The vast supply of primary information in fields that devote a large proportion of resources to research and development has made it virtually impossible for the R & D worker to scan all the primary information and select from it that which is of interest to him. As a result, a number of systems have been developed that supply reference information of various types that allow the R & D worker (among others) to cover his field of interest without having to search through all the primary sources and enable him to identify for purposes of retrieval the original material he desires to examine more fully.

The type of reference information provided by these systems is defined as secondary information, and it is secondary in the sense that it refers to and perhaps summarizes the primary information.

The different types of secondary information are:

1. Abstracts publications. An abstract generally contains a bibliographical description of a certain piece of primary information and a narrative describing in some way the contents of that piece of primary information. The narrative may be informative, in the sense that it contains some of the information given in the primary document, or it may be indicative, in the sense that it merely indicates what the primary document contains.

2. Titles lists. A titles list is so called because the main and often sole indication of the contents of the primary items it lists is given by the title. In a small number of cases the title may be "enhanced" by the inclusion of additional terms to further describe the subject content.

3. Enquiry-answering services. Secondary information may be supplied in answer to an enquiry in person or by telephone or mail. It should be noted that the enquiry-answering services that are provided by research associations and similar bodies tend not to be restricted to supplying only secondary information, but may also supply primary information, either in the form of published information or as an opinion of a subject expert.

4. Selective dissemination of information services. Services of this type generally scan the various sources of information and select from them secondary information related to particular fields in which the subscriber has stated he is interested. This selection of secondary information is sent to the subscriber at regular intervals. The information supplied may take the form of an abstracts or titles list but it differs from the first two classifications above in that these lists are tailored to meet the specialized interests of the individual subscriber.

5. Others. The information field is not static, and account has to be taken of any new forms of providing secondary information that are as yet not clearly specified.

The Information System

In the first instance the information system may be recognized by the fact that its output consists of one or more of the information services described above. This statement may appear platitudinous, but there is no simple method of identifying information systems as they function in a variety of environments and employ various methods of internal organization.

Situation. The conditions under which an information system functions are as follows:

1. In a library. The secondary information services may have developed as a result of library activities, or an information system and library may have been set up together; in either case the information system uses library facilities and the two often function together inextricably.

2. In a parent body. This will usually occur in a research association, learned society, or large firm. The information system usually will have access to the specialist employees within the parent body, and again the exact extent of the information system is difficult to determine. The information services may be regarded by the parent body as part of the overall service provided to members, or they may be run on a commercial basis.

3. Independently. Some information systems are situated on their own and are run as clearly differentiated production units. They may be part of a larger organization but the ties are not so close as in items 1 and 2, and there is not the same problem of determining the extent of the information system.

Structure. There are many ways in which the individual information system may be organized internally. For example, there may be a number of information staff of various levels who do all the secondary information work such as abstracting, and who also perform all necessary editing and proofreading. Alternatively, the information system may be more of a clearing house for selecting and distributing primary information to outside specialists who perform the abstracting and indexing, while the internal staff may concern themselves entirely with editorial functions. There are a range of alternatives between these two extremes whereby varying amounts of the information work may be contracted from outside. Similarly, the distribution of secondary information to users may be performed within the system or be carried out by the printer.

Thus an information system may assume a variety of different forms, although the form it takes and the environment in which it functions will not necessarily be reflected in its output; for example, all of these types of organization may produce a similar type of abstract.

Costs

Definition

The cost of production is the amount of resources, in money terms, that are utilized in the production of a specified output.

The exact determination of this cost can lead to difficult problems in cases where the information system is closely connected with some other service such as a library or where more than one output issues from the same set of resources. This means that the costing may take the form of a two-tier estimation procedure: the information system itself must be identified and the costs isolated for the various services produced.

The "real" costs of production may be described as those costs that ultimately would cease to exist were the particular output under consideration to be discontinued. This is almost equivalent to the costs that are directly and indirectly incurred by the production of secondary information and will be referred to as the marginal cost of producing secondary information. The calculation of this "real" cost in its entirety requires that certain allocations of joint costs of production be made, as well as the calculation or collection of the more direct and variable costs. As a consequence there is a point beyond which it must be stipulated that no costs are incurred with respect to the information system, for example, the top level of administration of the parent organization of which the information system is but one part and where there would never be a change in costs as a result of discontinuing the information system. The criterion to adopt with respect to the identification of the point beyond which costs are not pursued is to assess whether the activity being examined is directly related to the business of producing secondary information. This is one of the important instances in which discretion must be exercised.

Classification

In a cost-effectiveness study of information systems the initial costs that are required are (a) the total cost of the production of secondary information by the information system; and (b) the total cost broken down by type of output where more than one type of secondary information service is produced by the information system.

In the first instance it is possible to set out an exclusive list of the costs of producing secondary information. The first three classifications are treated as being the direct manpower cost and the remainder are treated as charges associated with the information system.

1. <u>Professional manpower</u>. This refers to the trained personnel who are concerned with the dissemination and retrieval of information and the utilization of information materials and sources. At times there may be difficulties in distinguishing between information staff and library staff.

2. <u>Clerical manpower</u>. These are the persons employed to perform typing, secretarial duties, and routine work. The degree to which clerical work encroaches upon information work varies widely between establishments, depending upon the standard of person employed and the organizational structure.

3. <u>Management</u>. The duties that come under this heading are organization, coordination, financial control, and personnel. In this case we are concerned only with direct management and this will normally exclude persons above the head of department in which the information system is situated. The rationale for this is that higher-level management costs arise mainly as a result of coordinating the information system into another structure, and this introduces an element of noncomparability when systems that are part of a larger organization are compared with those that function as an independent organization.

4. <u>Acquisition</u>. This is the cost of the material that is processed by the information system. In some cases literature is supplied free by publishers, or is received on an exchange basis, or perhaps the information staff travel to nearby libraries, and this cost is not always comparable between information systems.

5. <u>Printing</u>. Normally this is the bill received from a printer for a year's production, but in a few cases the printing is performed within the organization. In this case it is necessary to estimate the cost incorporating materials, machinery, and printing staff.

6. <u>Distribution</u>. This is normally performed by the printer and a bill may be obtained for the year. Otherwise, an estimate of the manpower and postage costs that are internally incurred must be made.

7. <u>Computer</u>. This will refer mainly to storage, sorting, and retrieval costs.

8. <u>Rent, rates, heat, light</u>. This is the normal cost of occupying premises and varies according to size, terms of tenure, and geographical location.

9. <u>Stationery, telephones</u>. These are normal office expenditures.

10. <u>Miscellaneous</u>. This includes all the relatively small items of cost that are not set out above, for example, advertising, depreciation of office equipment, office cleaning, etc.

These costs will give the total cost of the information system, and this is then split among the various services produced.

For the purposes of cost comparisons it is useful to split these costs down rather more fully, and the following classification of professional manpower input has been developed.

1. <u>Scanning</u>. The process of reading the original material and insolating those items that are to be processed and disseminated.
2. <u>Abstracting</u>. The work of transforming the original material into abstract form.
3. <u>Indexing</u>. The preparation of author and/or subject indexes.
4. <u>Editing</u>. The exact characteristics of this function vary between systems, but normally it is the checking of abstracts and indexes for terminology, relevance, and form.
5. <u>Proofreading</u>. This is the checking of galleys and page proofs that are prepared by the printer.
6. <u>Miscellaneous professional</u>. There are various tasks that are not included above, depending upon the organization of the system, for example, classification, listing, etc.

The Collection and Allocation of Costs

The previous section has set out the costs that are to be isolated and it is now necessary to explain the method of collecting and allocating the costs of the various classifications.

1. <u>Manpower</u>. This is the money paid to and on behalf of those persons engaged in the production of secondary information, according to the definition of professional and clerical manpower. This, therefore, includes not only salary but all associated costs such as national insurance (NI), Selective Employment Tax (S.E.T.), graduated pension, and superannuation.

The ideal method of allocating costs here can be set out in three stages.

a. Estimate the cost that would be incurred in producing each service or output on its own: this is CO_i ($i = 1, 2 \ldots i$), where i is the number of outputs
b. Calculate the assigned cost of each output; this is the cost of joint production minus the cost calculated in (a) for all outputs other than the one under consideration. The assigned cost of output 1 is

$$AO_1 = CO_{i+1} - \sum_{2}^{i} CO_i$$

where AO_1 = the assigned cost
CO_{i+1} = the cost of joint production

c. Gross up the assigned costs individually as follows:

$$(A_1 + A_2 + \ldots A_i) \frac{CO_3}{\sum_1^i A_i}$$

The alternative method of allocating this cost between the classification of activity is to calculate the time spent on each activity as a proportion of total working time and then multiply the salary cost by this proportion. Thus the cost of activity i is

$$\frac{C H_i}{H}$$

where H_i = the time spent on activity i during the period being costed
H = the total hours worked
C = the salary of the individual (corrected for NI, etc.)

By taking the time spent working as a base, the cost of spare time—for example, holidays, coffee breaks, etc.—is allocated among the various activities according to the proportionate time spent on each.

In order to make the results comparable it is obviously of importance to ensure that the estimation of the time spent on each activity by the individuals concerned is as accurate as possible. However, the same data and facilities for collection are not available in each system and it may be necessary to use several different approaches from time to time. These are listed in order of preference:

a. <u>Existing records</u>. In some cases records of time spent on various activities may have been kept, and the most useful form of this is those records that refer to the year being costed; if not, then discretion must be exercised in using those records that appear to be most appropriate.
b. <u>Production cycle</u>. In some cases, especially where a regular publication is produced, there is an established routine that is followed in each production cycle—usually one month. The staff may be willing to keep diaries of this period, but if not they are usually able to state quite accurately how their time is distributed during this cycle.
c. <u>Representative time periods</u>. In cases where there is no production cycle the staff may be willing to keep diaries. In this case they

should be kept for a series of single weeks spearated from each other by at least one-week intervals, and an attempt must be made to ensure that these weeks are as representative as possible.
d. <u>Subjectivity</u>. None of the above methods may be possible and it will be necessary to rely entirely on the individual's estimate of how his time is distributed. All possible efforts should be to use any other available information on the production process in order to check on these estimates.

Where possible all of those methods should be used because it is important to find out if there are significant differences between the estimates of individuals and the actual distribution of time.

2. <u>Machinery costs</u>. It will be found that only a small proportion of systems perform their own printing, which is the main area in which these costs arise.

The first problem in this case is to determine the cost that is relevant to the period being costed. This cost is composed of maintenance and estimated capital consumption in a year. The first of these may be ascertained from the bills paid, but the second is estimated in a fairly arbitrary manner; this is to find the purchase price of the machine and obtain an estimate of its useful life and scrap value, which gives an estimate of the capital consumption for the "average" year. This is the straight-line method of calculating depreciation, and although there are a number of other methods available with their own particular claims to sophistication, the simple method is considered adequate in this context. The yearly cost is then maintenance plus depreciation.

Where the machinery is used in the production of more than one output, it will be necessary to allocate this cost between them. This can be approached in the same way as the allocation of salary costs, that is, using calculated and assigned costs (see item 1 above). If this procedure is not possible then the costs should be allocated on the basis of the proportion of operating time spent on each activity. The four methods of assessing the time spent on each activity are, in order of preference: existing records, production cycle, representative time periods, and subjectivity. The same comments apply to these methods as in the manpower case.

3. <u>Management</u>. Normally the cost of management does not lend itself to a treatment similar to that of manpower because it is necessary to manage a production unit as a whole and it is often impossible to state that a particular management activity is related solely to one output. However, it may be necessary to ascertain how much of the cost of management is relevant to the production of secondary information—this is the case where the information system is part of a larger organization—prior to allocating this cost to the various secondary services produced.

There are three bases upon which the cost of management may be allocated: (a) according to the number of persons employed on each output; (b) according to the direct wage cost of each output; and (c) according to the total money cost of each output exclusive of management.

Where possible, one of these methods should be used to isolate the cost of management relevant to secondary information; otherwise it is necessary to rely on a subjective estimate. The above three methods may then be used to allocate the cost of management between the different services produced in order to test for any significant differences that may appear.

It should be noted here that for the independent, single-service information system none of the above problems apply.

4. <u>Centralized overheads</u>. It can occur that the information system being costed is part of a parent institution that is composed of several information systems, research laboratories, libraries, and so forth, and there is a central office responsible for the general management of the overall conglomeration. It is often asserted that the individual information system should bear a part of this centralized overhead and this section is concerned with the criteria upon which to base the allocation of this cost.

It must be stressed here that we are concerned with the determination of the costs of producing secondary information, and thus the cost of all the activities of the central office that are not devoted to this end must be excluded. The costing procedure here is essentially functionally oriented.

In the first instance, then, it is necessary to estimate how much of the central office is attributable to the production of secondary information. In the absence of meaningful records of the time spent on various activities it normally will be necessary to rely on subjective estimates here. Once the portion of the centralized overhead relevant to the production of secondary information has been isolated, it is necessary to move to the second stage of the problem, which is the allocation of this cost between the various information systems. At this point the assertion is made that there are five more or less exclusive activities that the central office may perform on behalf of the information system. The determination of these costs will again be a matter of subjectivity in most cases, and it is necessary to discuss each type of cost briefly and set out the criteria for allocation.

a. <u>Coordination</u>. This is the planning of the work and areas of each information system to avoid duplication and overlap and the bringing together of systems when projects of mutual interest are undertaken. This cost will be allocated to each information system in proportion to the total cost of each.

b. <u>Finance</u>. Here the accounting framework is dealt with, decisions on expenditure are made, and financial services such as salary payments may be provided. This cost will be allocated according to the total cost of each information system as in (a).
c. <u>Marketing</u>. This is the selling function of the central office and will include the creation of goodwill. The allocation of this cost between information systems can be based on two types of data: the rate of growth of sales, and the value of sales. The first of these has many drawbacks, for example, a big sales effort may be made to arrest declining sales, while in the second case no account is taken of the fact that marketing costs are incurred now in the expectation of a future return. The method that will be adopted is to allocate the cost in proportion to the total sales value of each information system.
d. <u>Personnel</u>. This includes selection of staff and manpower planning. This can be allocated according to two principles: the number of persons employed in each information system, and wage costs in each information system. The second of these is to be used whenever possible, as the personnel commitment is likely to vary with the level of staff employed as well as the absolute number.
e. <u>Troubleshooting</u>. This is the assignment of personnel in the central office to investigate and deal with problems of production that arise and cannot be handled locally. There are three possible methods of approach to allocation here: (i) subjective estimates; (ii) according to the number of managerial staff in each information system; and (iii) according to the value of the second method in each information system. The third of these is to be used whenever possible, with the second as second choice.
f. <u>Other (specify)</u>. There may be cases where the above are not exclusive and the method of allocation will depend to a great extent on the nature of the activity.

    5. <u>Data base</u>. In some systems a data base is built up continually and may be used in the production of more than one service, for example, abstracts and enquiry answering. The yearly cost of building up this data base is allocated between services on the basis of the proportionate total manpower costs of each service. The reason for adopting this procedure is that this basis is most likely to reflect the actual input of the data base into the production process of the information system.

    6. <u>Rent, rates, heat, light</u>. Where the information system is part of a larger organization and is housed in the same premises then the portion of these costs applicable may be approximated by using the floor space of the information system that can be allocated between the different services produced using the most comprehensive

indicator of the capacity usage of the premises; this is the proportion of all other costs relevant to each service.

7. <u>Acquisitions</u>. This is the money paid for the primary and secondary information used in the production of the secondary services. It is not always possible to collect this cost because, as already indicated, not all of the information used is necessarily paid for. Furthermore, where the information system is attached to a library and the material is also used for library purposes then it is difficult to establish a principle for allocating the cost between the two. The approach to adopt here is to collect this cost whenever possible in order to obtain an indication of what it would cost to buy all the literature covered.

8. <u>Office equipment</u>. This is the depreciation on the various office items used by the staff of the system. An inventory is taken and the replacement costs found; an arbitrary life span of five years is then assumed and the straight-line depreciation calculated. This cost is allocated between different services according to the distribution of time of the individuals who use the items.

9. <u>Telephone, postage, etc</u>. If no separate bills are available for these items then approximations may be made by using the number of calls made and letters sent.

Costs and the Time Period

Normally, costs are collected for the last financial year for which figures are available, and this raises the problem that in many cases the time distributions for the present year are used and this may affect the results where there have been changes in organization or personnel between the past and the present. Where such changes are so great as to make the time allocation procedure impossible, then an attempt should be made to perform the costing for the current year using the past year as a guide and incorporating the changes according to discretion.

Where costs have been collected for different years for the various systems it is necessary to standardize these for the purpose of comparison. This can be done by using the index as in the Annual Abstract of Statistics for salaries, wages, prices of materials, and prices of fuel.

The Collection of Costs

The first and most important step is to obtain the cooperation of the establishment. It has been found that a successful method of doing this is first to write a letter giving a description of the nature and aims of the study and suggesting that a member of the research team visit the establishment to discuss the matter further. This member of the team can then proceed to sell the project to the establishment as well as he is able. He can at the same time assess the likely number of man days required to complete the study.

Once cooperation has been obtained, the activities of the person performing the costing operation will be largely as follows:

1. Discuss requirements with department head and present a list of the detailed costs required, which will usually have to be extracted from records—a questionnaire for this purpose is shown at the end of this appendix—see p. 144. By this stage it should have been ascertained which of the four methods of assessing manpower and machinery time distribution is to be used.

2. Determine which type of services are produced and in what form; the department head usually will give a description of the production process and this should be taken down in detail.

3. Interview each member of staff separately and obtain a full idea of which functions and activities each performs. This interview may also provide the subjectivity basis for computing time distribution. Even if subjectivity is not to be used in the final analysis, it is still of interest to see how far the subjective estimates agree with the work records. The person's qualifications and experience should also be noted.

4. Where machinery is used in the production process, ascertain the function for which the machinery is used and obtain estimates of the time devoted to the production of each output (even if detailed records are available).

5. Draw up a flow chart of operations and show this to the department head for verification. Ensure that there are no gaps in the flow and that no activities have been omitted. If necessary discuss what steps are necessary to fill any gaps.

6. If the accounts are available then go through these as a check. Certain allocations of "overheads" may have been made and these should be treated with caution.

7. Go through the flow chart systematically with the estimates of time distribution in order to make sure that a complete picture has been obtained. Any apparent anomalies that arise here should be referred to the department head. An example here is the case where it takes perhaps three days in the month for a particular part of the process to be completed, but the persons concerned each allocate, say, five days of their time per month to this activity.

8. Having collected all the costs that appear to be relevant, and having checked the allocations as far as possible, obtain the agreement of the department head to write for clarification of any difficulties that may arise in writing up a report.

9. Throughout the period of the visit, note should be taken of any points that appear to be relevant with respect to noncost aspects (see the following section).

Noncost Aspects

There are a number of aspects of the information system that may affect the quality of its output, and this will not necessarily be reflected in the data on the number of items processed in a specified time period. These aspects will be referred to as noncost aspects and are, in particular, the type and quality of the secondary information service provided and the quality of the staff employed in the service.

It is expected that, in general, the noncost aspects will be included in the overall assessment of effectiveness. However, the separate collection of data on these aspects is required so that they may be used in the analysis of the results and in providing explanations for differences in cost-effectiveness. In addition, the data will be essential where there is only one secondary information service in a discipline or industry since it will, in that case, be difficult to attribute differences in cost-effectiveness to differences in quality of service rather than to differences in discipline or industry.

So that an indication may be obtained of these noncost differences between information services, data should be collected as applicable, under the heads listed in the Noncost Questionnaire—see p. 145.

The Costing Report

There are three main reasons for compiling a cost report in a fixed format for each information system: (a) it serves as a check that all costs have been included; (b) it can be submitted to the information system for confirmation; and (c) it is useful to have a full explanation of any irregularities that may affect the comparability of the results.

The report will normally contain these four parts:

1. <u>Description</u>. This will summarize the information system and give an outline of the production process and an examination of the services produced. Any problems encountered will be discussed, the type of data available will be explained, and the basis upon which costs were allocated will be discussed.

2. <u>Tables</u>. These should be set out according to the classification in the section entitled "The Collection and Allocation of Costs," and the cost per abstract, or enquiry, and cost per subscriber calculated for each heading, together with percentages.

FIGURE C.1

Flow Chart: Abstracting Services,
Production of Monthly Abstract Journal

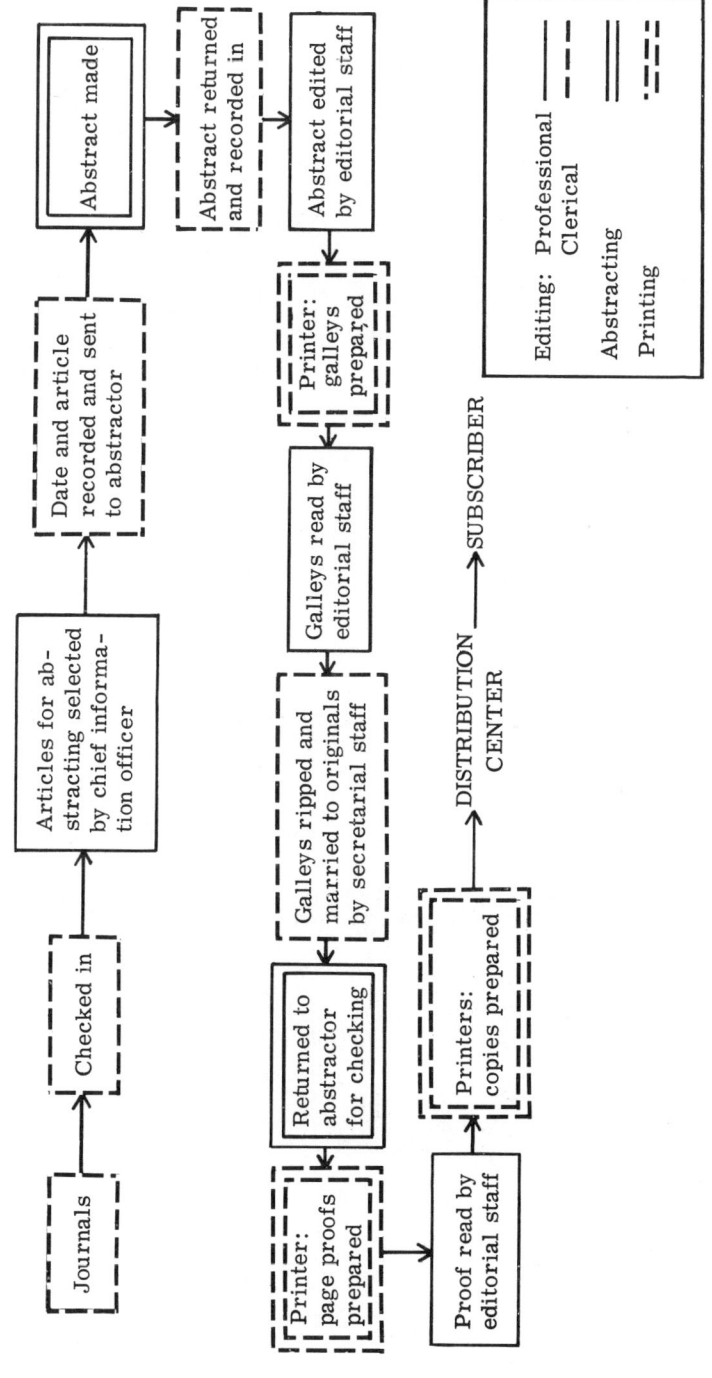

3. <u>Flow chart</u>. The procedure of drawing up flow charts has various objectives in this case: (a) to ensure that the method of producing secondary information in the establishment is fully understood; (b) to ensure that no costs are missed out; and (c) to supplement in a visual form the detailed description of the operation of the information system. The first two items are here served by the rough flow charts drawn up during the costing exercise, while (c) is the more refined version that goes into the report, an example of which is given in the Cost Questionnaire on pp. 144 and 145. In order to increase the degree of visual information, those areas of activity that are associated with particular cost classifications are further identified as in Appendix Figure C.1, and a key to these classifications is compiled.

4. <u>Noncost aspects</u>. These will be covered by the Noncost Questionnaire on p. 145, and any further aspects that may affect the quality of the service of the particular information system will also be noted at the discretion of the individual.

Cost Accounting and the Economist's Costs

The procedures set forth in this manual are specifically designed to assess costs for the purpose of the calculation of cost-effectiveness and have been approved by the consultant cost accountant.

It should be noted here that in the fields of accounting and cost accounting the figures that are collected and their presentation are greatly influenced by the uses to which the costs are to be put: the data collected for the purposes of drawing up a profit statement are different from those required for cost control purposes. This being the case, it is possible that the costs collected under the procedures of this manual may not be of great help in areas of analysis outside those for which they are specifically intended.

Cost Questionnaire

1. (a) Salary and wages list
   (b) National insurance
   (c) Private pension scheme
2. Where costs are incurred externally please state
   (a) Fees   (i) Abstracting
              (ii) Indexing
              (iii) Other (please specify)
   (b) Printing costs
   (c) Distribution costs
   (d) Computer costs
   (e) Other (please specify)

3. Machinery
   For each item please state
   (a) Date of acquisition
   (b) Cost of acquisition
   (c) Expected date of replacement
   (d) Maintenance charges
   (e) If possible, please estimate present scrap value and replacement cost
   (f) Rental costs
4. Subscriptions
   (a) Journals
   (b) Other information services
   (c) Books
5. Advertising
6. Rent, rates, heating, lighting
7. Telephone, telex, postage
8. Stationery
9. Transport and general expenses
10. Other charges (cleaning, etc.)

Noncost Questionnaire

Type and Quality of Service

Content of Output Items
   Title   Index terms
   Author   Citations
   Bibliographic Reference   Other (specify)
   Abstract

Abstracts (if included)
   Abstract copied from original paper if available (edited if necessary)
   Abstracts specially prepared,
       by staff of service
       by external abstractors
       indicative
       informative

If Listing
   Arrangement by broad subject classes:
       or alphabetical by author
       or alphabetical by first title word
       or by title of periodical
       or chronological

    or random
    or other (specify)

<u>Typography</u>
   Range of fonts
    or upper and lower case only
    or upper case only

<u>Indexes</u>
   Subject: Conventional or key word in context (or variants)
   Author
   Other (specify)
   Frequency (specify)

<u>Timeliness</u> (where known, or readily ascertained)
     Period between publication of primary document and publication of item in secondary service
and/or Period between publication of item in secondary service and publication of subject index
or   Period from receipt of request by service to receipt of answer by the user.

<u>Quality of Staff</u>

For each nonclerical staff member, list:
 (a) Scientific or technical qualifications
 (b) Scientific or technical experience
 (c) Information or library qualifications
 (d) Information or library experience

APPENDIX D

INFORMATION EFFECTIVENESS
STUDY MANUAL

Introduction

The Department of Economics at the University of Edinburgh has been commissioned by the Office for Scientific and Technical Information (OSTI) to undertake an investigation of the economics of information systems. The investigation has taken the form of a cost-effectiveness study of the methods by which scientific and technical information is transferred to persons who are engaged in applied R & D work. Scientific and technical information is both an input to and an output of research and development. It is with the former aspect that we are concerned. Research and development can be undertaken without the assistance of information about research and development that is currently taking place or has taken place in the past in the same and related fields. This is likely, however, to involve a high probability that duplication of R & D work will take place. Similarly, if R & D work in a given field is carried out with the aid of the maximum amount of available information in that field, precious little R & D output may be achieved because the major part of the R & D worker's time may be taken up with reading and literature searching. In other words, information can never completely replace research and development nor can it be regarded as a prerequisite of research and development. The question is really one of how much information, and in what form it should be presented to R & D workers.

This study is an attempt to take an initial step toward answering the questions of how and how much; and to develop a methodology that can be used in later investigations to provide the answers. It should be remembered that this study is an economic exercise and that an investigation of the relative cost-effectiveness of different information systems will allow a judgment to be reached about how efficiently resources are allocated in the field of information production.

For practical purposes the study has been split into two parts, an information costing study and an information effectiveness study. This manual is concerned with the effectiveness aspects of the study. The objective of the effectiveness study has been interpreted as assessing the degree to which the information needs of persons in the field of applied research and development are satisfied by the products of different information systems. Again, for reasons of practical convenience, limits have been imposed on the types of scientific and technical information being considered. First, only formal, as opposed to informal, information systems are being studied. An informal method of transferring information—for example, by word of mouth between friends—might not only be difficult to locate, but also difficult to cost, and is accordingly excluded from consideration. In addition, only secondary, as opposed to primary, scientific and technical information is included within the confines of the investigation.* We are thus concerned with the effectiveness of the products of formal secondary scientific and technical information systems.

Secondary Information Services†

An information system may be described broadly as method by which information is produced. However, the information user is probably less interested in the method of production of the information he uses than with the form of the product of the information system. Thus in order to assess the degree to which the information users needs are satisfied it is necessary to examine the product rather than the method of production. The product of the information system is known as an information service.

The vast supply of primary or original information, particularly in fields that devote a large amount of resources to research and development, has made it virtually impossible for the R & D worker in these fields to scan all the primary material and to select from it that which is of interest to him. As a result a number of services have been developed that supply reference information generally covering particular subject fields in a broad fashion. This amounts to an attempt to allow the R & D worker, among others, to cover his field of interest without the burden of having to search through all the relevant primary sources and to allow him to identify and retrieve original material he desires to examine more fully.

The type of reference information provided by these services is known as secondary information. It is secondary in the sense that by referring to and perhaps summarizing the primary information such information appears in a form that is secondary to the original

---

*An explanation of the differences between primary and secondary information is given in the following section.

†The reader should from this point take for granted that references to information services or systems cover only those that are formally produced.

source. Primary information may be described as the material contained in original journal articles, books and reports, published and unpublished. Secondary information is information that refers to primary information. This reference generally includes a bibliographical description and may also contain summary information about the contents and aims of the primary information.

Secondary information usually takes the form of either an abstract or a title. These appear more commonly in published form but they may also appear as duplicated lists, or they may be provided in the form of an enquiry answering service conducted by telephone or mail.

Secondary information services are produced by a number of different sources. Some sources exist solely to produce secondary information on a commercial basis. In other cases the production unit forms an adjunct to some professional establishment such as a research association or a learned institute or society, each of which is generally directly connected with a scientific discipline or subject field(s) by way of existing to serve members (firms and individuals who have an interest in these fields). The third major category is the production unit that is run on a commercial basis but provides secondary information in addition to primary information.

A check sheet* that is attached to Part One of the questionnaire (a copy of which is included as an appendix to the manual), classifies a number of the different forms in which secondary information is produced. These are:

1. Published abstracts. An abstract generally contains a bibliographical description of a certain piece of primary information and a narrative describing in some way the contents of that piece of primary information. The narrative may be informative, in the sense that it provides some of the information contained in the primary item, or it may be indicative in the sense that it briefly describes the contents of the item. Abstracts may appear in a number of different forms and these are listed in the subdivisions of the heading "abstracts." Pure abstracts refers to the provision of abstracts without the addition or supplement of any primary information. Abstracts in this form are usually indexed and consequently are important tools for retrieving information in a particular field that may have appeared some time in the past. Abstracts may also appear as a section contained in a primary journal or a report, and since these may form an important source of secondary information, account must be taken of them. These may also be indexed.

---

*The check sheet is included in the questionnaire but this appears elsewhere and is not duplicated here.

2. <u>Published titles</u>. A "title" comprises a bibliographical information describing an item of primary information. A title differs from an abstract in that the former does not contain a narrative summary of the content of the primary information. Generally secondary information of this form appears as a list of titles that is designed to keep the reader abreast of new developments in his own and related fields. This is known as current awareness. As a result, titles lists are not generally regarded as being useful information retrieval tools and are not usually indexed.

3. <u>Enquiry-answering services</u>. Secondary information in the form of an abstract or a title may be supplied in answer to an enquiry, either by telephone or mail. It should be noted that the enquiry-answering services that are provided by research associations and similar bodies tend not to be restricted to supplying only secondary information, but may also provide primary information.

4. <u>Selective dissemination of information services.</u> Services of this type generally scan the various sources of information and select from them information related to particular fields in which the subscriber has stated he is interested. This selection of information is sent to the subscriber at regular intervals. The information supplied may take the form of an abstracts or titles list but it differs from the first two classifications above in that these lists are tailored to meet the specialized interests of the applied research or development worker.

5. <u>Others</u>. The information field is not static and account has to be taken of any new forms of providing secondary information that are as yet unknown.

An indication has been given of the existence of a wide variety of secondary information services. Many of these cover the same subject field although they differ in the breadth and depth of coverage. In such a situation an investigation of relative effectiveness of the different services that are produced is likely to be of value in determining whether the allocation of economic resources in the field of secondary information is the most appropriate one.

The Survey

The objective of the study is to assess the relative effectiveness of formal secondary scientific and technical information services in the field of applied research and development. In addition there are the concomitant subsidiary objectives of generating data and developing an analytical methodology. The means being adopted to achieve these objectives is to carry out a survey of firms and individuals engaged in applied research and/or development work.

The survey may be divided into three distinct but related stages. These are the formulation of a questionnaire, the sampling procedure, and the use of the questionnaire in the sample field.

Formulation of a Questionnaire

A description of the formulation of the questionnaire is not entirely relevant to this manual, since this stage of the survey has already been completed. However a brief indication of what is involved may be useful as background information.

The formulation of a questionnaire is influenced largely by the type and quantity of data and other information that is to be obtained, and also by the method of analysis to be adopted. In the present study the formulation of the questionnaire and the development of a methodology went hand in hand and were of mutual benefit to one another. This was done practically by means of a number of pilot surveys and the discussion of the results of these surveys by members of the research team. The end result was the formulation of a questionnaire that contained a set of questions aimed at producing measurements of the relative effectiveness of different secondary information services and that had been subjected to extensive testing in the field of applied research and development.

Sampling Procedure

In order to generate the data required for the analysis, it is necessary to communicate in some way with the firms and the individuals within these firms who are engaged in applied R & D work. Ideally each firm and each individual concerned with applied R & D work should be sampled. This is not usually practically feasibly because not only may there be a large number of firms, but there is also likely to be, in at least some of the firms, a large number of applied R & D Workers.

The procedure to be followed to reduce the number of firms and individuals to be sampled to manageable proportions will be determined to some extent by general principles that should be followed in the selection of a sample. Perhaps the most important is that the sample population should as far as possible accurately reflect the statistical characteristics possessed by the total population from which the sample is drawn. In order to achieve this it would seem helpful to consult a relevant text.*

---

*See, for example, C. D. Moser, <u>Survey Methods in Social Investigation</u> (London: Heinemann, 1958).

Use of Structured Questionnaire in the Sample Field

In order to obtain measures of the effectiveness of information services, it seems desirable to approach the users of that information there are two fundamental ways of making this approach; by letter or by personal contact.

Having devised the questions, it was seen that the length of the questionnaire and the complexity of some of the questions would render a satisfactory response rate by mail, at best, unlikely. In addition, in order to ensure unambiguous replies, personal interview was considered preferable. This approach also permits the easy collection of peripheral information regarding the information habits of research workers.

In the collection of data from questionnaires such as this, it is important to ensure complete accuracy and consistency in the way in which the questions are asked. Therefore, it was decided to use a fixed-format rather than a free-format questionnaire. The essence of the fixed-format questionnaire is that each question is asked only as it is printed and only in the order in which it is printed. The use of prompts and duplicate questions must also be standardized and used only as described in the following section of this manual.

The interviewees are the budget allocator, the librarian or information officer, and several research workers. It is desirable that arrangements for interviews are arranged in advance of the visit to the firm by the interviewer. This will save time in identifying who is to be interviewed.

The budget allocator is the person responsible for allocating the share of the establishment's budget to the provision of secondary information services. He generally will be the research director or equivalent, but in those firms where there is no organized R & D department, he may be the chief engineer or the managing director. It is important that an arrangement to interview the budget allocator be made by the interviewer prior to his visit. This may help to ensure his availability, because he tends to be an extremely busy person, and will certainly enable problems of identification to be solved in advance. In some firms budgeting decisions are made by a committee or by the board of directors. If it is not possible to interview the decision-making group as a body, advance warning will allow arrangements to be made for members of the decision-making group to be interviewed.

In many firms the identification of the librarian or information officer will be straightforward. Some firms, however, may use one of the research team as organizer of secondary information. In cases of doubt, the librarian or information officer is the person responsible for the administration and organization of information services. He is not the person who deals with the press or is responsible for publicity or public relations, etc. As can be seen from the questions asked of him, he must have knowledge about the information services purchased by the firm. It may be necessary to interview more than one person where, for example, responsibility for acquisition of information services is separate from that for dissemination of the information, as might be the case where there is both a librarian and an information officer within a single firm. Again it can be seen that advance arrangements are likely to be desirable.

The Questionnaire

The purpose of this section is to describe and explain the function and content of the questionnaire. As was indicated in the previous section, the interviewer should not deviate in any way from the content of the questionnaire. In each interview it should read out the exact wording of the introduction, and of each question in the relevant part of the questionnaire, to the interviewee. If the interviewee does not understand a question, the question should be repeated. If the question is still not understood, the interviewer should prompt the respondent by explaining the purpose of the question as outlined in the notes below. Again, if the respondent does have difficulty in comprehending a question or is slow to answer, he should not be hurried or prompted by the interviewer until he indicates that he either does not understand the question or is unable to answer the question for some other reason. If after prompting and allowing a reasonable interval to pass still no answer is forthcoming the interviewer should avoid embarrassing the interviewee by persisting with the question and should move on to the next question. He should note the reason, if any, for inability to answer. At all times the interviewer should exercise patience, tact, and respect. He should also endeavor to put the interviewee at his ease by attempting to achieve a smooth flow in the reading out of the questionnaire content and by avoiding stiltedness and abruptness.

The questionnaire consists of three parts, which are designed to elicit information from persons who perform three distinct functions. These are the information officer or librarian, the research director or budget allocator, and the research worker. These functions may be carried out by different individuals or they may overlap in the sense that one person may perform two or more of them. The information that will be obtained from the answers given by these persons will include the raw data that will provide measures of effectiveness of different secondary information services plus supplementary information necessary for classifying and analyzing the raw data.

The following notes are intended to aid the interviewer's understanding of the reasons why certain questions are asked and, where necessary, to allow the interviewer to explain the question to the interviewee. In addition to reading and understanding this manual and the each interviewer should familiarize himself with the environment in which he will be carrying out the field work. This might be done by carrying out a number of pilot interviews in firms that do not appear in the sample, and also by familiarizing himself with the names and contents of formal secondary information services by visiting scientific and technical libraries and speaking to librarians.

The interviewer should be aware that information services are produced in different forms and may appear as a printed publication, a duplicated list, or an enquiry-answering service conducted by telephone or letter. The conditions to be met are that such a service provides secondary scientific and technical information and that it is recognized as a formal, as opposed to informal, method of information transference. A further distinction arising is that the secondary information service may be produced within the establishment (internally) or may be obtained from a source outside the establishment (externally). In addition the service may supply both primary and secondary information, as, for example, a journal that contains both original articles and a section devoted to secondary information in the form of a list of abstracts or titles.

The following comments relate to specific parts of the questionnaire and give an outline of the reasons why particular questions are being asked and, in certain cases, issue instructions to be carried out by the interviewer.

Part One: Information Officer or Librarian

It is not always the case that there is a person of either of the above titles within the establishment. For example, the function of information officer may be carried out by a librarian, or a director, or the chief engineer, etc. Given that the primary objective of the questionnaire is to elicit information, the title of the person being interviewed is relatively unimportant provided he or she is responsible for or is knowledgeable about the acquisition and use of scientific and technical information within the establishment.

Where there is no information officer as such, the nearest proxy should be interviewed. Identification of this person will generally have been made in advance of the interview.

Introduction: The introductory paragraph is intended to furnish the interviewee with a brief outline of the objectives that underlie the survey and the fields being covered. The introduction should be read out verbatim to the interviewee and care should be taken to ensure that the interviewee understands how secondary information is defined for the purposes of the survey.

Name of Establishment: Because some establishments have similar names, the full name of the establishment should be clearly stated.

Question 1: This question and the following question are designed to obtain estimates of the demand for and supply of secondary information within the establishment.

The information being obtained in the first part of the question is an essential contribution to the analysis of the data generated by the survey and the interviewer should endeavor to obtain as precise a figure of the number of persons engaged in applied R & D work as possible. Those persons who work on the fringes of applied research and development, such as laboratory assistants or draftsmen, should be excluded as should those engaged only in pure research. If, however, a person who carries out pure research also engages in applied research and development, he should be included. In other words, any person who engages in applied R & D work, either full time or for only part of his work week, should be included as one member of the total applied R & D work force within the establishment.

Staff refers only to information and library staff whose function is wholly or partly to acquire and/or to provide information to employees within the establishment. If in an average interval of time, say a week, the period devoted to information work by such staff is less than the duration of the full working week this person(s) should be designated part time. In order to express a part-time staff member in terms of a full-time equivalent, the proportion of the working week spent on information work should be calculated and stated.

Question 2: List of information services: Only formal services providing secondary scientific and technical information should be listed. If the interviewer is required to make an on-the-spot decision about whether to take account of a service that provides both secondary and primary information he should include only those services of which a part is explicitly devoted to the provision of scientific and technical secondary information. Where the establishment is a subsidiary part of a larger firm that provides a secondary information service to the establishment, such a service should be explicitly identified as an external service. Similarly, all internal secondary information services should be identified as such.

An internal secondary information service may be defined as the production of secondary information from a source within the establishment additional to the secondary information services obtained from outside the establishment. It should be noted that the external services may be utilized in the production of the internal service.

Check Sheet: The check sheet that is attached to the back of Part One of the questionnaire gives a general classification of the different types of secondary information service that are taken by an establishment and should be given to the information officer to aid him in identifying the relevant external and internal services under the classified headings that the establishment acquires or provides.

Check List: The interviewer should write the names of the relevant internal and external services under the classified headings given on the check list as they are identified by the information officer.

Subscriptions: The corresponding purchase price of each service should be inserted on the check list. If the service is free or in part of a subscription to a research association or similar body, this should be made clear by inserting "free" or "subscription" in the appropriate column of the check list.

Question 3: The purpose of this question is to identify those services that are important to the establishment in terms of value of information content and/or use. This information will be used in question 9. If there are more than four services given, the interviewer should limit the answer to the four most important services.

Question 4: Question 4 is designed to obtain an estimate of the value of the secondary information services that form an input in the production of an internal secondary information service. This information will supplement information on value obtained in Part Three of the questionnaire as well as allowing an estimate of value added in the production of the internal service from the combination of inputs.

Question 4(a): Total cost relates to the provision of an internal secondary information service of the type listed on the check sheet. This covers cost of all inputs including manpower, rental and operating costs of machinery and equipment, stationery, plus the cost of any external secondary information services that may be used as inputs. It does not include the cost of running a library or the purchase prices of primary and secondary publications that are not used as inputs. Where the information staff perform functions in addition to provision of the internal service, a proportionate estimate of salary costs based on proportion of time spent on provision of the internal service in an average year should be taken.

Question 4(b): By "relative values" is meant the relative contributions of internal and external inputs to the total value in terms of use of the internal service. The interviewer should ensure that comparison is made between the group of internal inputs and the group of external inputs, and not between individual inputs. It should be clearly understood that "external inputs" refer only to those external secondary information services that contribute to the production of the internal service. "Internal inputs" refer to all other factors that are used in providing the internal service.

Question 4(c): In this question the interviewee is asked to compare the values of individual external secondary information services that are used in the production of the internal secondary information service. The answers should be entered in the check list.

Question 5: The purpose of this question is to discover whether the respondent considers the information needs of the establishment are being met under present conditions. If they are not, and financial constraints arising from, for example, poor trading conditions, or government pressure, are assumed to disappear, the question attempts to find out what steps if any would be taken to satisfy these needs by increasing the number of external secondary information services and/or information staff. Budget refers to total amount of annual expenditure on provision of information within the establishment, including direct and overhead costs. Staff refers to information workers only.

Question 6: This question follows on naturally from the previous question and also acts as a check to ensure that the purpose of increased expenditure on external secondary information services is not merely to meet inflationary price rises.

Question 7: The purpose of this question is to arrive at an indication of how the pattern of behavior of the establishment as a purchaser of secondary information services would change as a result of a large cut in total expenditure on these services by the establishment. Because of the indivisibility of individual services, the measures envisaged by the information officer librarian may not exactly equal 10 percent. The interviewer should not be concerned about this as long as the cutback is approximately 50 percent. If there is a wide divergence (say $> \pm$ 15 percent) this should be noted.

The interviewee may find difficulty in answering this and the following four questions partly because of their hypothetical nature and partly perhaps because the interviewee might not be responsible for making the decision to arrive at the answers to these questions. Because it is a difficult question, the interviewer should avoid the temptation to save time by prompting the respondent. If after a reasonable interval the respondent is still reluctant to answer the question, give a prompt by stating "What we are after is what you yourself would do if you were faced with this hypothetical situation. Your answers will be treated in strictest confidence."

The services that would no longer be purchased should be entered in the appropriate column on check list number 2.

Question 8: This question is similar in purpose to the previous one except that instead of a cut in expenditure taking place, an increase in price is postulated in an attempt to obtain an indication of how price change will influence the pattern of purchases. There is a further difference, in that the price rises may result in an increase in expenditure. This will tend to depend largely on the flexibility of the individual establishment's financing arrangements within a given year.

The answers to this question should again be inserted in check list number 2.

Question 9: This question is designed to produce an estimate of the cost of obtaining from alternative sources the secondary information used in the given services if these services were no longer available.

For the two parts of this question, the interviewer should use the services identified in question 3. These generally will amount to no more than four. For additional services the interviewer should apply his own discretion, choosing services that appear in the list of sample publications relevant to the study. No more than three or four services should be included under each classified heading. It should be noted that the heading "abstracts" includes all classes of abstracts.

Question 9(a): This question is designed to find out what the cost to the establishment would be if the establishment itself were to set about providing from alternative sources the secondary information contained in the given services the establishment uses. The interviewer may find the respondent has difficulty answering. This may be a result of inability to think of a method of assessing cost. In such a situation use the following prompt: "The cost of providing information from alternative sources will tend to be determined largely by the employment of additional staff to scan and select from primary journal articles plus the cost of purchasing additional information services. Could you give an estimate of the cost by assessing the number of additional staff, etc., that would be employed?" If this prompt is used the interviewer should make a note of it.

Question 9(b): If the respondent again finds difficulty in answering, the interviewer may find it necessary to explain as follows: "Price tends to be an important determinant variable in the decision to purchase a given commodity, but it need not necessarily indicate the true value of the commodity to the buyer, who may be prepared to pay considerably more. In view of this, could you indicate the price at which you would stop buying each of the services?" The confidential nature of the information given may also require emphasizing. The prompt should again be noted, if it is used.

Question 10: Where an establishment obtains a secondary information service from a research association or a learned society, this service is usually received in return for a membership subscription. This subscription may entitle the member to a number of services in addition to the secondary information service, and the purpose of this question is to arrive at an estimate of the proportion of the subscription that might be attributed to the cost of purchasing the information service alone. If the respondent is unable to answer after a due interval of time, use the same prompt as is given in Question 7. If the prompt is used this should be noted.

The answers should be entered in the appropriate column on check list number 2.

Question 11: The aim of this question is to identify substitute secondary information services and to ascertain whether a change in price in any one of them would result in a decision to purchase that one. Where a change in price would induce the purchase of one or more of the substitutes, answers should be entered in check list number 2.

Part Two: Research Director or Budget Allocator

The person(s) to be interviewed will be responsible for approving the level of expenditure on information/information section within the establishment. This person tends to vary in status between establishments, and may be anyone up to the managing director. This person(s) will usually have been identified prior to the visit.

Introduction: The interviewer should introduce the budget allocator to the effectiveness study by reading out the introductory paragraph, again ensuring that the respondent is clear about the way in which secondary information is defined. The situation may arise where verbal communication with the budget allocator is difficult, for example, if he is seated at the opposite side of a broad desk. The interviewer in such a position should hand the budget allocator the copy of the questionnaire that is attached to the back of Part Two. This should help to overcome any difficulties of this nature.

Question 1: The first two parts of this question are designed to obtain information about the level of total expenditure on information and to ascertain whether formal budget estimates are carried out or whether the annual level of expenditure is arrived at by less formal means.

Question 1(a): The budget referred to is the total annual expenditure on the provision of information by the establishment, including staff and overhead costs. If there are no formal budget estimates made, an approximation of the current annual level of expenditure should be obtained.

Question 1(b): If the answer is negative, ascertain how the budget level is determined, and by whom, and note this on the questionnaire.

Question 1(c): This question is similar in purpose to question 5 in Part One, but the wording has been altered in the light of results obtained from earlier pilot surveys. Note that the question refers to secondary information services only and not to other items of expenditure.

Questions 2, 3, 4, 5: These questions duplicate questions 7, 8, 9, and 10 in Part One and reference should be made to the notes on these questions. The principal reason for asking a duplicate set of questions is to endeavor to obtain answers to these questions where no answers have been given in Part One. This situation may arise where the interviewee in Part One did not have sufficient knowledge or responsibility to be able to give an answer. In addition, where answers can be obtained to these questions in both Parts One and Two, it might be expected that these would not be identical in viewpoint and that valuable information describing management attitudes might be obtained.

The interviewer should use his discretion when submitting these questions. The budget allocator may have insufficient knowledge to be able to consider secondary information services separately from other aspects of information provision. If this is the case the interviewer should record a brief description of the method by which decisions concerning changes in expenditure on <u>secondary</u> information services are reached, and who has the responsibility for making such decisions. A note should also be made of the reason given for inability to answer the question.

In question 4, the same services as were named in question 9 of Part One should be used.

Part Three: Individual Member of Staff

Introduction: Apart from outlining the background to the study, an important function of reading the introduction is to enable the interviewee to relax. To assist this, the interviewer should try to avoid reading out the contents of the questionnaire in a stilted manner and should attempt to maximize the flow from the introduction to and between the questions.

Name of Establishment: See Part One

Question 1(a): The purpose of this question is to ensure that the interviewee satisfies the criteria for being in the sample. The interviewer should ensure that the sample individual is aware of the distinction between pure and applied science. Pure science may be defined as work undertaken for the advancement of scientific knowledge without a specific practical aim in view. If, after clarification, the answer to the question is "pure science" the interview should be terminated. If possible a replacement should be obtained, one who satisfies the criteria of being a member of the sample population. If, however, the interviewee engages in both pure and applied research and development, the interview should continue. It should be made clear to the interviewee that the questions being asked concern only his applied R & D work and no other type of activity.

Question 1(b): The answer to this question contributes a vital part to the measurements of effectiveness. By "working week" is meant an average week under current working conditions. The interviewer should ensure that the respondent takes account of time spent on related information work when stating that proportion of his working week is spent on applied research and development.

Question 1 (c): The purpose of this question is to provide information by which respondents may be classified, thus permitting greater depth in the analysis of the results. "Field of interest" refers to applied R & D work only.

Question 2: The reason for this question is the same as for 1(c). The respondent may have difficulty in recalling exactly how many years he has been engaged in applied R & D work, and accordingly the interviewer should not press for a precise answer.

Question 3: The purpose served by this question is twofold. The respondent is acquainted with the terms "current awareness" and "information retrieval" and their respective definitions, and in the second part of the question information is obtained that is used in calculating the effectiveness value of different services.

Question 3(a): The interviewer should attempt to ensure that the respondent clearly understands the difference between current awareness and information retrieval. He should be made aware that the need for current awareness information is here defined as a continuous need covering the respondent's subject fields of interest while the information retrieval need will, in the context of a given problem, tend to occur once only.

The paragraph appearing between questions 3(a) and 3(b) should be read out verbatim to the respondent.

Question 3(b): It should be noted that information needs refer to needs met by secondary information only.

Question 4: This question is designed to allow identification of the various secondary information services the respondent uses and the needs they are designed to satisfy. The answers to each part of the question should be entered in the check list. It is essential to list the name of each service as accurately and as clearly as possible in order to allow identification at a later date.

Question 5: The purpose of this question is to elicit information that can be used in the measurement of value. The question is presented in two stages in an attempt to reduce the complexity of calculation required by the respondent to produce an answer.

The interviewer should note that the first section concerns not only secondary but all types of information, while the second section is confined to ascertaining what proportion of the answer to the first section is devoted to secondary information. It is essential in order to avoid confusion that the answer to part (b) should be expressed in terms of part (a) and not as a proportion of total R & D work.

Question 6: This question is intended to identify the relative importance of secondary information services as a source of secondary information in the respondent's R & D work.

Trade literature: Magazines and other publications of that type, the contents of which are primarily concerned with advertising the products of firms within a particular trade.

Personal contact: A source of information produced by informal verbal contact between individuals. It should be noted that visitors to the establishment who act as a source of secondary information should be classified under personal contact outside the establishment.

Question 7: The secondary information services to be named in answer to this question are for use in question 10. Where four or less than four services are given, the respondent should be requested to name the four services he most uses. If he is unable to do so, all services should be recorded.

Question 8: This question is intended to identify substitute secondary information services that might be used to meet the respondent's respective secondary information needs.

Question 9: The answers to this question are used in conjunction with information obtained in the following question to produce a measurement of effectiveness. A brief explanation of what is covered by each listed characteristic is given below:

Speed in publication of secondary information or speed in reply to enquiry: The time interval that occurs between the publication of primary information and the appearance of secondary information that refers to that primary information. In the case of an enquiry-answering service or a service that permits a search to be carried out, speed is taken to be the time interval between submitting an enquiry and receipt of the answer.

Coverage of field of interest: The extent to which a particular secondary information service covers the sources of primary information relating to a given subject field.

Relevance to your need: The degree to which the secondary information provided by a service is relevant to an information need arising from applied R & D work in a given subject field. Despite the close relationship between coverage and relevance, the interviewer should not be deluded into thinking that the two are identical. The degree of relevance may be determined by the extent of coverage of primary information sources, insofar as irrelevant information will be supplied if irrelevant sources are covered. To that extent there is an overlap. However, even if coverage is 100 percent, irrelevant information may still be supplied. For example, information that was of considerable age is unlikely to be relevant for a current awareness need, or secondary information provided in a publication designed for chemists may not be of great relevance to the information needs of an engineer, although the latter may find it of considerable interest because it satisfies his sense of curiosity.

Degree of detail in content of information supplied: This will be determined largely by the amount of information given by the unit of information supplied, such as an abstract or the reply to an enquiry. At one extreme there is a little that supplies only bibliographical information while at the other there is an informative and illustrated abstract.

Subject arrangement or classification: The format or the way in which the contents of a publication are set out by subject field. This should not be confused with indexing.

Indexing: An index is an alphabetical list of key words (subject index) and/or names (author index) with corresponding reference or page number that allow an information user to refer to information about a particular subject based on keyword(s) or to refer to work by a particular author. The index generally relates to published information and may appear within the publication or be published separately. In addition, certain secondary information publications have annual and/or cumulative indexes that are a combination of the indexes relating to the individual issue of the publication over a given period of time.

Supply of additional services from the same location: There are cases where an establishment such as a research association, in addition to supplying published abstracts, provides an enquiry-answering service that backs up the abstract service. The provision of more than one related secondary information service from a single location may have certain advantages such as being able to tap a supply of specialized knowledge with a certain degree of convenience.

After reading the introductory paragraph to question 9, the interviewer should hand the respondent the check sheet containing the list of characteristics for ease of reference.

Question 9(a): It is essential that the respondent is quite clear about the distinction between this part and the following part of the question. This part is concerned with the characteristics that any secondary information service should possess in the eyes of the respondent, that is, the ideal situation. The second part applies to the group of services the respondent at present uses, that is, the situation as it actually is. This question should be asked separately for each information need and should be presented in two stages. The respondent should first be asked to indicate which characteristics he regards as being important before being asked to mark these important characteristics on a scale from 1-10 where 10 is the highest degree of importance. The interviewer should insert a check mark in the corresponding box in the appropriate column to indicate the important characteristics, and should then insert in the same boxes the corresponding scale mark. This procedure should be repeated for each information need.

Question 9(b): The interviewer should focus attention on a particular need and then ask the respondent to rank the characteristics of the given services he would like to see improved. The interviewer should insert in the appropriate box the corresponding ranking number beginning with "1," this indicating the characteristic most urgently in need of improvement. This procedure should again be repeated for each need.

Question 10: The purpose of this question is to furnish information that will contribute to one of the measurements of effectiveness.

The interviewer should make use of the answers given in question 7, identifying the most-used services, and question 4(b), ascertaining for which needs these services are used. The names of the most used services should be inserted beside the numbers i-iv in the first-row box containing the characteristic relating to speed. The corresponding numbers i-iv in the subsequent rows can then be used to refer to the given services without the need for rewriting the names of the services. The procedure to be followed is similar to that of the previous question in which each need is considered separately. For each need the respondent is requested to indicate the degree of satisfaction with each characteristic given by each of the most-used services. Where a given service is used to meet only one need, for example, current, the answers to be inserted in the other columns will be left blank. Again if a given service does not possess a characteristic—for example, if an abstracting service is not indexed—the answers will be zero for each need for which it is used for that particular characteristic.

Question 11: This question is designed to produce a measure of the total value of the secondary information used by the individual and to provide a means by which this total value may be attributed to individual secondary information services.

The respondent should accordingly be made aware that the question refers only to the various secondary information services that he uses. The answers to part (b) should be inserted in the final column of the check list.

Question 12, 13, 14: The purpose of these questions is explained in the paragraph immediately preceding question 12. This paragraph should be read to the respondent.

Question 12: Before the respondent can answer this question he will generally have to consider what he would in an identical situation to the present but where no secondary information services were available. For example, he might attempt to obtain the same amount of information by reducing his leisure time or by reducing his applied R & D time, or at the other extreme he might limit the amount of information he obtained. Each of these will tend to result in a cost to the respondent either in terms of leisure time or job satisfaction or both. His behavior will be determined largely by how much importance he attaches to secondary information.

Because the respondent may require time to consider the question, the interviewer should exercise patience and tact. If, however, the respondent is unable to answer the question in its present form the interviewer should prompt him by explaining as follows: "If the services you use now were no longer available to you you might either carry on as before and obtain a smaller amount of secondary information in a given time or you might attempt to get the same amount of secondary information as before by working longer hours. This might cause you a loss in leisure time and a reduction in job satisfaction. In either case could you estimate the value of the loss, if any, to you personally?" If this prompt is used it should be noted at the end of the question.

Question 13(a): The answers given by the respondent may take the form of a certain number of hours or may be expressed as a percentage of either total R & D work or of the working week. The interviewer should ensure that the answer given, in whatever form, is expressed in unambiguous terms in order to allow conversion of the answer to a standardized code form and should if possible obtain an answer expressed in hours.

Question 13(b): This question should be asked only if the respondent has indicated in the preceding question that he will reduce his research time. The distinction between this and the previous question may have to be explained.

The difference occurs in the imposition in part (b) of the condition that research output or research progress is maintained at the same level as it was in the prior situation where secondary information services were available. The interviewer must again ensure that the answer is written down in unambiguous terms, and should if possible be expressed in hours.

Question 13(c): Weekly average number of hours refers to total number of hours the respondent devotes to work in an average week. This may not coincide with the working week of the establishment, if, for example, the respondent takes work home with him in the evening.

Question 14: This question is designed to find out how dependent the respondent is on secondary information services in order to carry out his applied R & D work. For example, a chemist may regard chemical abstracts and the other services he uses as vital and may assign a mark close to 50. Alternatively, he may use these services only because they are freely provided and would not feel inconvenienced if they disappeared. In the second case, the mark assigned would tend to be very small. The interviewer may have to explain the question by quoting the examples given above.

Question 15: The salary figure furnished by this question is of vital importance in several of the methods of measuring effectiveness. Year of birth is used for classification purposes.

If the respondent is unwilling to indicate his rate of salary, the interviewer should tactfully explain the confidentiality of the information and the fact that the information given by the respondent will be rendered anonymous when it is immersed in the information obtained from other respondents. If the respondent appears reluctant to give his salary figure verbally it may help to prompt him by asking "Would you like to write your salary figure here?," at the same time proferring the pen to the respondent. If this is unsuccessful the interviewer should attempt to obtain an approximation of the salary rate or ask for the interval on the salary scale on which the respondent at present lies.

Summary

This manual has attempted to describe the objectives of the information effectiveness study and to explain the means by which these objectives are to be attained. In particular it is concerned with the generation of data.

The background to the study was outlined in the first section. There the objective of the study was indicated as being to carry out an economic investigation of the relative cost-effectiveness of formal secondary scientific and technical information services. The second described how secondary information services operated and the various forms in which they appeared, while in the third section, the method being adopted to generate data that will permit the assessment of the effectiveness of secondary information services was explained briefly. This method was split into three interrelated stages—sampling procedure, formulation of a questionnaire, and the use of the questionnaire in the sample field. There is a fourth stage, the analysis of the results, but this does not properly concern this manual and is being treated separately. The fourth section gave a detailed treatment of the questionnaire, including the reasons for including certain questions and suggestions as to how the different parts of the questionnaire should be submitted in interview.

The generation of data by use of a questionnaire in interview can lead to considerable error in the data collected, arising from bias or inconsistency in response, or even nonresponse to questions. In order to minimize the risk of such error, the interviewer should at all times avoid embarrassing or flustering or intimidating the interviewee. While a certain degree of informality is probably desirable, an impression given to the interviewee of a frivolous attitude on the part of the interviewer may lead to answers that lack thought and may lack meaning. The interviewer, in order to avoid potential sources of error, should at all times exercise judgment, tact, and patience.

When the survey has been completed, the results of the survey will be analyzed. This analysis will produce information that will allow conclusions to be reached whereby the relative effectiveness of information systems can be judged. Such information, however, is not wholly meaningful without consideration of the costs of producing the various information services. When the results of the effectiveness study are combined with the results of the corresponding costing study, sufficient data should be at hand to allow judgments to be made about the cost-effectiveness of information systems and the degree of efficiency in the allocation of resources in the information field.

ABOUT THE CONTRIBUTORS

J. N. WOLFE was born in Montreal, Canada, and was educated in Montreal schools and at McGill University, the University of Glasgow and Oxford University. He was a lecturer at the University of Toronto from 1952 to 1960 and Professor of Economics at the University of California, Santa Barbara from 1961 to 1964. He has been Visiting Professor at the University of Rochester, Purdue University and the University of California, Berkeley. He is the author and/or editor of numerous books and articles in learned periodicals and has been economic consultant to the British and Canadian governments and director of many research projects for government and scientific foundations and industrial associations.

DONALD H. BRYDON is Assistant Investment Manager of Airways Pension Scheme, the funded pension scheme of British Airways. Mr. Brydon holds a B.Sc. in Mathematical Science from the University of Edinburgh and spent three years as a Research Associate in the Department of Economics at Edinburgh.

ALEX SCOTT is Research Associate in the Esmee Fairbairn Economics Research Centre, Heriot-Watt University. Most of his research has been in the field of efficiency in the non-market sector, and he has published work on the demand for housing and various aspects of research into education. Alex Scott holds the degrees of M.A. and M.Sc. from the University of Edinburgh.

RALPH YOUNG, formerly a research associate with the Department of Economics, University of Edinburgh, is at present an executive research officer with the Bureau of Agricultural Economics, Canberra, Australia. At Edinburgh his research work included a thesis on the determinants of demand for the public library lending service. His published work includes a number of articles which have appeared in the Quarterly Review of Agricultural Economics, and Applied Economics, and a contribution to the report "The Central Borders - A Plan for Expansion" Mr. Young holds an M.A. and M.Sc. from the University of Edinburgh.

THOMAS M. AITCHISON is Deputy Director of INSPEC, the International Information Services Division of the Institution of Electrical Engineers which provides information services to the physics and engineering communities. Mr. Aitchison has been some 25 years in information work, initially as information officer in various sectors of industry. In recent years he has been particularly concerned with the development of computer-based information dissemination and retrieval systems. He has contributed to various conference proceedings and is the author of a number of research reports and of articles in <u>Aslib Proceedings, NERC Review, Information Storage and Retrieval, Physics Bulletin</u> and <u>Program</u>. Mr. Aitchison is a Bachelor of Science of St. Andrews University, an Associate of the Library Association and a Fellow of the Institute of Information Scientists.

T
10.65
G7
W64

OCT 23 1975